Simply Delicious
THE COSTCO WAY™

Cherry-Peach Wonton Cups with Lemon-Mascarpone Cream can be found on page 197.

Simply Delicious
THE COSTCO WAY™

Delectable dishes using Costco products

Stephanie E. Ponder
Editorial Director

With a foreword by
Tim Rose and Jeff Lyons

Issaquah, Washington

Senior Vice President E-commerce and Publishing:	Ginnie Roeglin
Publisher:	David W. Fuller
Editorial Director:	Stephanie E. Ponder
Art Director:	Doris Winters
Associate Editorial Director:	Tim Talevich
Associate Art Director:	Lory Williams
Associate Editor:	Judy Gouldthorpe
Senior Designer:	Brenda Shecter
Photographers:	Darren Emmens Ryan Castoldi
Food Stylists:	Amy Muzyka-McGuire Christine W. Jackson
Kitchen Manager:	Linda Carey
Studio Assistant:	Nicole Soper
Business Manager:	Jane Klein-Shucklin
Advertising Manager:	Melanie Woods
Assistant Advertising Manager:	Kathi Tipper
Production Manager:	Pam Sather
Prepress Supervisor/Color Specialist:	MaryAnne Robbers
Assistant Production Manager:	Antolin Matsuda
Online Editor:	David Wight
Print Management:	James Letzel and Ayako Chang, GSSI
Distribution:	Rossie Cruz

FIRST EDITION
Printed by Toppan Leefung Printing (Shanghai) Co., Ltd, Shanghai, China
ISBN-13: 978-0-9819003-4-6
ISBN-10: 0-9819003-4-8
Library of Congress Control Number: 2012913114

Contents

*All food photographs by Iridio Photography,
Seattle, Washington, with the following exception:*
Iggy Ruggieri: Unilever, page 160

To Our Valued Members

We are delighted to offer you a gift—the 11th annual book in *The Costco Way* cookbook series—in time for the holidays to thank you for your business and your loyal membership. This book has been made possible through the support of Costco's many food suppliers.

As in past years, we've asked our suppliers to develop recipes that showcase products of theirs that we sell at Costco. A new twist this year is the "In the Kitchen With" pages, which give suppliers a way to share some of their personal favorite recipes and also speak to the quality and versatility of their products.

Returning in this edition is our special "Chef's Choice" section in the middle of the book. It features recipes from many of our favorite celebrity chefs, such as Melissa d'Arabian, Tom Douglas, Ree Drummond and Marcus Samuelsson. These top chefs have worked their magic to develop recipes using their favorite ingredients from Costco.

If you are watching your calories, not just your budget, many recipes are accompanied by nutritional information. And if you occasionally also have an eye on the clock, look for the "Quick & Easy" logo to find fast and delicious recipes that require minimal effort when your schedule is a little tight.

The secret of all the great dishes, old and new, featured in this book is top-quality ingredients. When you purchase your ingredients from Costco, you know you are getting the best—and at a great price.

We hope you enjoy *Simply Delicious The Costco Way* and that you try out our recipes with your family and friends. You can also find our past years' cookbooks online at Costco.com. Just type "Costco cookbooks" in the search window on our home page.

Bon appétit from all of us at Costco.

Ginnie Roeglin
Senior Vice President,
E-commerce and Publishing

Foreword

As we head into the second decade of our *The Costco Way* cookbook series, it's a great time to reaffirm Costco's buying philosophy. We strive to offer the highest quality at the lowest possible price, providing our members with unparalleled value. We work with suppliers who are just as passionate about the items they provide to Costco members as we are. That collaboration between buyers and suppliers is a significant part of the value equation.

Regardless of trends or fashionable ingredients, our job at Costco is to continually improve the products our members purchase and better define the attributes of quality for each item. From premium trim specifications to higher grades and superior freshness to larger sizes, Costco buyers know what it takes to deliver a first-rate product.

And we've seen time and time again that you, our members, are able to identify quality and value. One of our greatest joys—and proof of your savvy shopping skills—is overhearing a member relate his or her positive experiences with a product to another member. Most members seem more than happy to help their fellow shoppers by talking to them about their favorite items, based on taste, quality and price. This doesn't occur just in the warehouse either. At nearly any gathering or social event, someone will be singing the praises of a recent culinary success made possible with the help of Costco.

The recipes in this cookbook are meant to give you the opportunity to create your own kitchen masterpieces. All of the recipes have been kitchen tested, giving you greater confidence and peace of mind when deciding what to cook. Whether you're entertaining guests or cooking for family, we are sure you will find that these recipes taste as good as they look. And whether it's your favorite ingredient prepared in a new way or a dish featuring something you've never considered trying before, we hope *Simply Delicious The Costco Way* will become the go-to source for your new favorite, show-stopping recipes.

Tim Rose
Senior Vice President,
Foods and Sundries

Jeff Lyons
Senior Vice President,
Fresh Foods

About This Book

Welcome to the 11th annual cookbook in *The Costco Way* series.

As with our earlier books, *Simply Delicious The Costco Way* will be handed out to members on a first-come, first-served basis the weekend after Thanksgiving as a token of our appreciation for their membership.

And as with Costco itself, the format of the book remains simple and direct. The book is arranged with sections for breakfasts, appetizers and beverages, salads and soups, side dishes, entrées and desserts.

The index at the back of the book contains listings by recipe and food item. We also have included a "Supplier Listing" section with contact information for all of the participating food suppliers.

Every recipe has been identified with the supplier's name and logo. We want to thank each of these suppliers for their support of this book. (Please note that some branded products may not be sold in your part of the country. In such cases, you should substitute a similar product.)

Again this year, some of the recipes have nutritional information listed with them. This is helpful for anybody watching calories and following a controlled, healthful diet.

Our popular "Chef's Choice" chapter offers 37 pages of recipes developed by some of the country's most accomplished chefs. All of these chefs have achieved national or international renown with cookbooks of their own, television shows and/or exceptional restaurants. Thanks to all of them for helping to make this another exciting addition to *The Costco Way* cookbook series.

Please enjoy this year's recipes, aimed as always at making your home-cooked meals simply delicious.

David W. Fuller
Publisher

Simply Delicious
THE COSTCO WAY™

Breakfasts

Holiday Apple and Sausage Breakfast Casserole

Columbia Marketing International

1 pound pork
  breakfast sausage

2 CMI Granny Smith apples,
  cored and chopped

5 tablespoons sugar, divided

1 teaspoon ground cinnamon

6 cups cubed French bread,
  toasted in the oven until
  light brown

3 cups shredded
  Cheddar cheese

9 large eggs, beaten

⅔ cup sour cream

1 teaspoon vanilla extract

½ teaspoon salt

3 cups milk

Coat a 12-by-9-inch baking dish with nonstick cooking spray.

Brown sausage in a small skillet, stirring to crumble.

Toss apples in a bowl with 2 tablespoons sugar and cinnamon.

Place half of the bread cubes in the prepared baking dish. Top with half of the sausage, half of the apple mixture and half of the cheese. Repeat the layers.

In a medium bowl, whisk together eggs and sour cream. Whisk in 3 tablespoons sugar, vanilla and salt. Add milk and whisk until combined. Pour over the mixture in the baking dish. Cover with plastic wrap and refrigerate overnight.

Preheat oven to 325°F.

Bake, uncovered, for about 70 minutes, or until a knife inserted in the center comes out clean. Makes 8-10 servings.

Recipe courtesy of chef David Toal of Ravenous Catering, Wenatchee, Washington.

Southwest Sausage Bake

Jimmy Dean

12 links Jimmy Dean Fully
  Cooked Turkey Sausage,
  coarsely chopped

1 red bell pepper, chopped

1 4-ounce can diced green
  chiles, drained

1½ cups (6 ounces)
  shredded low-fat Mexican
  cheese blend, divided

1 cup reduced-fat all-
  purpose baking mix

1 teaspoon ground cumin

1 cup fat-free milk

½ cup light sour cream

2 cups egg substitute
  (or 8 eggs, beaten)

Salsa and additional
  sour cream, for serving
  (optional)

Preheat oven to 350°F. Lightly grease a 13-by-9-inch baking dish.

Layer sausage, bell pepper, green chiles and 1 cup of the cheese in the baking dish.

In a large bowl, combine baking mix and cumin. Add milk and mix until blended. Stir in sour cream and egg substitute, mixing until blended. Pour over the sausage mixture.

Bake for 30-35 minutes, or until a knife inserted in the center comes out clean. Sprinkle with the remaining ½ cup cheese. Let stand for 10 minutes before serving.

Cut into 12 pieces. Serve with salsa and sour cream. Makes 12 servings.

Cuties Cinnamon Spice French Toast with Citrusy Syrup

Cuties California Clementines

4 large eggs
¾ cup milk
1½ teaspoons
  grated Cuties zest
1 tablespoon honey
¼ teaspoon
  ground cinnamon

¼ teaspoon
  ground nutmeg
8 slices French bread
Butter or pan spray
4 Cuties, peeled and
  sliced, for serving

CITRUSY SYRUP

Grated zest and juice of
  2 Cuties clementines
¾ cup real maple syrup
2 tablespoons honey
1 tablespoon butter

Prepare the syrup: In a small saucepan, combine zest, juice, maple syrup and honey. Bring to a boil and cook for 1 minute. Whisk in butter. Reduce the heat to very low and keep warm.

Prepare the French toast: Whisk together eggs, milk, zest, honey, cinnamon and nutmeg. Pour into a baking dish. Lay the bread slices in the egg mixture and let sit for about 30 seconds to absorb the batter, then flip over. The goal is to use up all the egg batter.

Melt some butter in a large nonstick skillet (or use pan spray) over medium to medium-high heat. Add as many slices of soaked bread as will comfortably fit. Cook about 2-3 minutes on each side, until golden and cooked through. Repeat with the remaining bread slices. (You can keep your French toast warm in a 300°F oven while you cook the rest.)

Serve warm, topped with sliced Cuties and drizzled with Citrusy Syrup. Makes 4 servings.

Recipe developed by Kathy Casey Food Studios for Cuties.

Croissant French Toast with Caramelized Bananas and Walnuts

Vie de France

2 large eggs
¼ cup milk
1 teaspoon ground nutmeg
1 teaspoon ground cinnamon
Vanilla extract, to taste
Salt, to taste
Vegetable or canola oil, for the griddle
1 Vie de France butter croissant, sliced in half

TOPPING

1 teaspoon butter
3 tablespoons light brown sugar
¼ cup (3 ounces) walnut pieces
1 ripe banana, sliced in half lengthwise
3 tablespoons orange juice
Pinch of ground cinnamon

In a shallow bowl, beat eggs, milk, nutmeg, cinnamon, vanilla and salt.

Heat a lightly oiled griddle over medium-high heat.

Place each slice of croissant in the egg mixture, soaking both sides. Place in the pan and cook both sides until golden. Move each half to a plate.

Prepare the topping: Melt butter in a sauté pan over medium-high heat. Add brown sugar and walnuts, then lay the banana slices in the pan, cut side up. Cook for about 20 seconds, then add orange juice and cinnamon. Turn the bananas carefully and cook for another 20 seconds.

Place the bananas and walnuts on the croissant halves, drizzling sauce from the pan on top. Makes 2 servings.

Baked Orange French Toast

Seald Sweet/South African Summer Citrus

2 large eggs
¾ cup milk
2 teaspoons vanilla extract
1 tablespoon sugar
Pinch of ground cinnamon
Butter, for frying
½ loaf French bread, cut diagonally into 8 slices
3 South African oranges, peeled and segmented
Pinch of sugar
Maple syrup, for serving

FILLING

1 cup part-skim ricotta
¼ cup fresh-squeezed orange juice
2 tablespoons sugar
2 large eggs
2 teaspoons grated orange zest

Preheat oven to 375°F. Butter an 8-inch glass pie plate.

In a bowl, combine eggs, milk, vanilla, sugar and cinnamon; blend well.

Melt butter in a skillet over medium-high heat. Dip bread into the batter and coat well. Cook for 1-2 minutes, then turn and continue cooking until lightly browned on both sides. Arrange the cooked slices in the prepared pie plate.

Prepare the filling: In a bowl, combine all ingredients and blend well. Pour over the toast slices.

Bake for 15 minutes. Arrange orange segments on top. Sprinkle the oranges with sugar. Return to the oven for 20 minutes, or until the fruit is hot. Let stand for 5 minutes. Serve with maple syrup. Makes 2-4 servings.

Nutella-Stuffed French Toast

Nutella

**4 slices brioche bread,
at least 2 inches thick
(or cinnamon, cinnamon
raisin or egg bread)**

**½ cup Nutella
hazelnut spread**

2 large eggs

1 cup 1% milk

½ teaspoon vanilla extract

**2-3 tablespoons
vegetable oil**

1 cup fresh berries

Preheat oven to 375°F.

Cut a slit in the side of each bread slice to make a pocket. Pipe or spoon 2 tablespoons Nutella into the center of each bread slice.

In a bowl, whisk eggs until smooth, then whisk in milk and vanilla.

Pour the egg batter into a shallow dish. Lay a filled slice of bread in the batter and let soak. Turn and repeat. The bread should be slightly wet but not soggy or falling apart.

Meanwhile, heat oil in a nonstick skillet over medium heat. Place the batter-soaked bread in the hot skillet and cook for 1½ minutes on each side, turning once, until golden brown.

Transfer to a sheet pan and bake for 5-6 minutes, or until heated through.

To serve, top each piece of stuffed French toast with ¼ cup fresh berries. Makes 4 servings.

Banana Walnut Pancakes

Splenda

**2 tablespoons Splenda
No Calorie Sweetener,
granulated**

⅓ cup reduced-fat milk

1 large egg

**1 cup pancake or
baking mix**

½ banana, mashed

**¼ cup walnuts,
finely chopped**

Cooking spray

In a bowl, mix Splenda, milk, egg, pancake mix, banana and walnuts until blended.

Spray a skillet with cooking spray and heat over medium heat.

Pour ¼ cup of batter per pancake into the pan.

Cook until the pancake surface begins to bubble. Flip and cook until done, about 2-4 minutes. Makes 4 servings (8 pancakes).

Splenda

Cinnamon Pancakes with Maple Cream Cheese Glaze

Kirkland Signature/Olde Thompson

1½ cups flour

1½ teaspoons baking soda

2 tablespoons sugar

2 teaspoons Kirkland Signature
   Saigon cinnamon

½ teaspoon Kirkland Signature sea salt

1½ cups milk

2 large eggs

½ teaspoon vanilla extract

3 tablespoons butter, melted
   and slightly cooled

Butter for frying

MAPLE CREAM CHEESE GLAZE

4 ounces cream cheese,
   room temperature

¼ cup milk

¼ cup maple syrup

¼ cup confectioners' sugar, sifted

In a large bowl, combine flour, baking soda, sugar, cinnamon and salt.

In a separate bowl, beat together milk, eggs, vanilla and melted butter. Pour the wet ingredients over the dry and whisk just until combined.

Prepare the glaze: In a medium bowl, whisk cream cheese until smooth. Add milk and maple syrup; mix until blended. Add sugar and whisk until no lumps remain.

Heat a nonstick skillet or griddle over medium heat. Add about a tablespoon of butter to the skillet and spread with a paper towel, leaving a thin coating. Using a tablespoon, add batter to the skillet. Cook until small bubbles form and are beginning to pop and the underside is golden brown, 1-2 minutes. Flip and cook for another minute, or until the pancake is cooked through. Continue with the remaining batter, adding butter to the skillet as necessary.

To serve, spoon the glaze over warm pancakes. Sprinkle with additional cinnamon if desired. Makes about 48 silver-dollar pancakes.

Spinach Quiche
River Ranch Fresh Foods

3 tablespoons olive oil
1 cup diced onion
2 cups sliced mushrooms
⅓ cup water
6 cups coarsely chopped
  River Ranch spinach
4 large eggs
⅓ cup milk
Salt and pepper
6 ounces crumbled
  feta cheese
1 9-inch pie crust

Preheat oven to 375°F.

Heat oil in a sauté pan over medium heat. Add onions and sauté for 10 minutes. Add mushrooms and sauté for 5 minutes.

In a saucepan, combine water and spinach; cook over medium heat until wilted. Drain in a strainer and squeeze out all moisture.

In a bowl, beat eggs and milk until smooth. Add salt and pepper to taste. Stir in the spinach and the onion/mushroom mixture. Blend in cheese. Pour into the pie crust; cover the edges with foil.

Bake for 35 minutes. Remove the foil, then bake an additional 5 minutes to brown the crust. Makes 8 servings.

Wild Alaskan Salmon Quiches
Morey's

1 cup toasted bread cubes
1½ cups shredded mozzarella
2 portions Morey's
  Seasoned Grill Salmon,
  cooked and flaked
¼ cup chopped red
  bell pepper
¼ cup chopped green
  bell pepper
12 large eggs
1 medium Roma tomato,
  cut into 6 slices
2 tablespoons grated
  Parmesan cheese
3 green onions, sliced
Salt and pepper

Preheat oven to 375°F. Grease a 6-cup jumbo muffin pan.

Place a single layer of bread cubes in each cup. Add the following to each cup, distributing evenly: some of the mozzarella and all of the salmon and bell peppers. Top with remaining mozzarella. Make an indentation in the center of the cheese to form a well.

In a bowl with a pouring lip, beat eggs. Pour very slowly into each well, letting the egg distribute itself until the cup is full, without overflowing. Top with a tomato slice, Parmesan and green onions.

Bake for 25 minutes, or until a knife inserted in the center comes out clean. Remove from the oven and let stand for 2-3 minutes.

Serve immediately. Add salt and pepper to taste. Makes 6 servings.

Pomodoro Egg Bake

Cal-Maine Foods/Hickman's Family Farms/Hillandale Farms/Norco/NuCal Foods/Oakdell Egg Farms/Wilcox Farms

4 medium tomatoes
½ cup shredded Parmesan cheese, divided

4 eggs
2 tablespoons thinly sliced fresh basil
4 English muffins, split, toasted

Preheat oven to 350°F.

Cut the top quarter off each tomato. Scoop out the tomatoes, leaving a thick shell intact. Remove any liquid from inside the tomatoes with a paper towel. Place the tomato shells in an 8-by-8-inch baking dish.

Sprinkle 1 tablespoon Parmesan cheese into each tomato shell. Break and slip an egg into each tomato. Sprinkle basil over the eggs.

Bake in the oven until the whites are completely set and the yolks begin to thicken but are not hard, about 30-35 minutes.

Sprinkle the remaining cheese over the eggs. Serve with English muffins. Makes 4 servings.

Nutritional information: Each serving has 269 calories, 16 g protein, 32 g carbohydrates, 9 g fat, 193 mg cholesterol, 3 g fiber, 511 mg sodium.

Breakfast Yogurt Bowls
Dawn Food Products

2 Kirkland Signature blueberry muffins
½ cup old-fashioned rolled oats
¼ cup sweetened shredded coconut
¼ cup sliced almonds

3 tablespoons vegetable oil
2 tablespoons clover honey
¼ cup dried cranberries
½ cup fruit yogurt

Preheat oven to 350°F. Grease a baking tray.

With a paring knife, core the muffins, cutting 1 inch in from the edge and ¾ of the depth of each muffin. Remove the muffin cores and place in a small mixing bowl. Set the cored muffins on serving plates.

Crumble the muffin cores in the bowl. Add oats, coconut and almonds. Mix well. In a separate bowl, combine oil and honey. Add to the oat mixture and mix well.

Pour the mixture onto the prepared baking tray and toast in the oven for 10-15 minutes, stirring every 5 minutes to ensure even toasting. Remove from the oven and let cool completely, 30 minutes. Add dried cranberries and mix well.

To serve, fill the muffins with yogurt. Top with the granola. Makes 2 servings.

Granola Breakfast Muffins
Nature's Path Organic Foods

2⅓ cups Nature's Path Pumpkin Flax Granola, divided

1½ cups unbleached all-purpose flour

2½ teaspoons baking powder

½ teaspoon baking soda

¼ teaspoon salt

Egg substitute equivalent to 2 large eggs

1 cup vanilla low-fat yogurt

¼ cup vegetable oil, plus 1 teaspoon for greasing muffin tin

3 tablespoons agave nectar or maple syrup

½ cup dried blueberries or cranberries

Set oven rack in the center position. Preheat oven to 400°F. Grease a 12-cup standard muffin pan, or use paper liners.

Measure 2 cups granola into a large bowl. Stir in flour, baking powder, baking soda and salt.

In a medium bowl, lightly beat egg substitute. Blend in yogurt, ¼ cup oil and agave nectar (or maple syrup).

Stir the yogurt mixture and blueberries into the dry ingredients to create a lumpy batter; do not overmix. Distribute the batter among the muffin cups. Sprinkle the remaining ⅓ cup granola on the muffins.

Bake for 7 minutes. Turn the pan around and bake 4-5 minutes longer, or until a cake tester inserted in the center comes out clean.

Remove the muffins from the pan and cool on a rack. Makes 12 servings.

Blueberry Muffins
Pure Via

1 cup whole-wheat flour

1 cup all-purpose flour

2 teaspoons baking powder

½ teaspoon baking soda

¼ teaspoon salt

1 tablespoon grated orange zest

20 packets Pure Via sweetener

1 cup buttermilk

¼ cup vegetable oil

2 large eggs

1½ cups fresh or frozen blueberries

Quick or old-fashioned oats (optional)

Preheat oven to 400°F. Line 12 muffin cups with paper baking cups.

In a large bowl, mix together flours, baking powder, baking soda, salt, orange zest and Pure Via sweetener. Stir in buttermilk, oil and eggs; mix until just moistened. Fold in blueberries.

Divide the batter evenly among the muffin cups. Sprinkle with oats, if desired.

Bake for 20-25 minutes, or until light golden brown. Cool for 1 minute, then remove from the pan. Makes 12 muffins.

Nutritional information: Each serving has 150 calories (28% reduction from traditional recipe), 4 g protein, 21 g carbohydrates, 6 g fat, 37 mg cholesterol, 2 g fiber, 226 mg sodium, 4 g sugar.

Dark Chocolate Açai Blueberry Muffins
Brookside

1½ cups wheat bran
1 cup 2% milk
⅓ cup vegetable oil
1 large egg
⅔ cup lightly packed light brown sugar
½ teaspoon vanilla extract
1 cup all-purpose flour
1 teaspoon baking soda
1 teaspoon baking powder
½ teaspoon salt
1½ cups Brookside Dark Chocolate Açai Blueberry

Preheat oven to 375°F. Grease 12-16 muffin cups or line with paper baking cups.

In a bowl, mix together wheat bran and milk; let stand for 10 minutes.

In another bowl, beat together oil, egg, sugar and vanilla. Add to the milk/bran mixture.

Sift together flour, baking soda, baking powder and salt. Add to the milk mixture and stir just until blended. Fold in Dark Chocolate Açai Blueberry. Spoon the batter into the prepared muffin cups.

Bake for 18-20 minutes, or until a toothpick inserted in the center of a muffin comes out clean. Cool on a rack. Makes 12-16 muffins.

Peach Pecan Muffins
SunWest Fruit Company

2½ cups diced SunWest peaches
1¼ cups granulated sugar, divided
½ cup butter, room temperature
2 large eggs
4 cups flour, divided
4 teaspoons baking powder
1 teaspoon salt
1½ cups milk
¼ cup packed light brown sugar
¼ cup very finely chopped pecans
¼ teaspoon ground cinnamon
5 tablespoons cold butter

Preheat oven to 400°F. Grease or line 24 muffin cups.

Place peaches in a bowl. Mix in ½ cup granulated sugar.

In a separate bowl, cream ½ cup butter and remaining granulated sugar (¾ cup) for 3 minutes, until smooth.

Add eggs individually and beat for 2 minutes, until fluffy.

In another bowl, combine 3½ cups flour, baking powder and salt.

Fold the flour mixture and milk into the butter, egg and sugar mixture. Fold in the peaches. Pour the batter equally into the muffin cups.

In another bowl, combine ½ cup flour, brown sugar, pecans and cinnamon. Mix thoroughly. Add cold butter and mix by hand until crumbly. Sprinkle the muffins with the crumbles.

Bake for 15 minutes, or until golden brown. Makes 24 servings.

Walnut-Kiwi Bread
Regatta Tropicals

2 cups sifted flour

½ cup sugar

2 teaspoons baking powder

1 teaspoon baking soda

½ teaspoon salt

1½ cups chopped and drained Regatta Tropicals kiwifruit

¾ cup chopped walnuts

1 egg, beaten

¼ cup butter or margarine, melted

1 teaspoon vanilla extract

Cream cheese, softened, for serving

Preheat oven to 350°F. Grease and flour a 9-by-5-by-3-inch loaf pan.

Sift flour with sugar, baking powder, baking soda and salt into a large bowl. Add kiwifruit and walnuts, and mix well. Add egg, melted butter and vanilla. Stir until just blended.

Pour the mixture into the prepared pan. Bake for 60 minutes, or until a toothpick inserted near the center of the loaf comes out clean. Let the bread cool in the pan for 5 minutes, then remove it from the pan and set on a rack to complete cooling.

Serve in thin slices spread with cream cheese. Makes 10 servings.

Date Pecan Bread with Citrus Icing
SunDate

1 cup SunDate Medjool dates cut into pieces

1 teaspoon baking soda

½ cup butter, at room temperature

⅔ cup sugar

1 large egg

1 teaspoon vanilla extract

1½ cups all-purpose flour

½ teaspoon baking powder

½ cup pecans, chopped

ICING

¼ cup lemon juice

¼ teaspoon grated orange zest

1 cup confectioners' sugar

Preheat oven to 350°F. Grease and flour a 9-by-5-inch loaf pan.

In a saucepan, combine 1 cup water, date pieces and baking soda. Bring to a boil, then set aside and let cool.

In a mixing bowl, cream together butter and sugar, then add egg and vanilla. Blend in flour and baking powder.

Stir in the date mixture and pecans.

Pour into the prepared pan. Bake for 20 minutes, then reduce the temperature to 300°F and bake until golden brown, about 30 minutes, or until a toothpick inserted near the center comes out clean. Let cool for 15 minutes.

Prepare the icing: In a bowl, combine all the ingredients. Add water as needed to achieve the desired consistency.

Drizzle the icing on the bread. Makes 6-8 servings.

Apple Baked Oatmeal
New York Apple/Pennsylvania Apple

2 cups rolled oats
(old-fashioned oats)

1½ teaspoons
baking powder

¾ teaspoon salt

¼ cup chopped pecans

¼ cup raisins or
dried cranberries

2 cups diced Eastern
Jonagold or Empire apples

3 large eggs

2 cups milk

⅓ cup firmly packed
light brown sugar

½ teaspoon ground
cinnamon

Preheat oven to 325°F. Butter an 8-by-8-inch baking pan.

In a large bowl, mix oats, baking powder and salt. Stir in pecans, raisins (or dried cranberries) and apples.

In another bowl, whisk together eggs, milk, brown sugar and cinnamon. Pour over the dry mixture and stir to combine.

Pour into the prepared pan and bake in the center of the oven for about 1 hour, or until golden brown. Serve warm. Makes 6 servings.

Tip: This can also be baked ahead and reheated at 250°F for about 20 minutes, or until warmed through.

Hearty Walnut Oatmeal
Kirkland Signature/Diamond Foods

½ cup Kirkland Signature
walnut halves

1 cup old-fashioned oats

1 cup milk

1 cup cold water

Pinch of salt

½ cup half-and-half

2 tablespoons brown sugar

1 cup raspberries

Preheat oven to 350°F.

Spread walnuts on a baking sheet or in a shallow pan. Bake, stirring once or twice, until lightly browned and fragrant, 7-10 minutes, or toast walnuts in a small pan over medium heat, stirring occasionally.

In a small saucepan, combine oats, milk, water and salt. Bring to a boil over medium heat and cook, stirring, for 4-6 minutes, or until thick and creamy.

Spoon the oatmeal into 4 bowls. Top with half-and-half and sprinkle with brown sugar, raspberries and toasted walnuts, dividing equally. Serve immediately. Makes 4 servings.

Walnut Energy Bars (Gluten Free)
California Walnut Board

3 cups Kirkland Signature California walnuts, divided

1 cup dried cherries

1 cup dried Mediterranean apricots

½ cup honey

½ cup vanilla whey protein powder

½ cup rolled oats

2 teaspoons cherry extract

Preheat oven to 250°F. Line a baking sheet with parchment paper.

Set aside 1 cup walnuts. Place remaining ingredients in a food processor and process just until the mixture is sticky and holds together. Add the reserved walnuts and pulse on and off to coarsely chop.

Press into a 7-by-10-inch rectangle and cut into 20 equal pieces. Place on the prepared baking sheet and bake for 30 minutes.

Let cool, then transfer to an airtight container. Makes 20 bars. (Or cut into 1-inch squares for a more bite-size bar.)

Variation: Add 1 cup unsweetened flaked coconut. Reduce the cherry extract to 1 teaspoon and add 1 teaspoon coconut extract.

Grape-Peach Breakfast Crumble
Divine Flavor

3 cups baking mix

½ cup agave nectar or granulated sugar

½ cup milk

3 cups Divine Flavor grapes cut into ¼- to ½-inch pieces

3 cups Divine Flavor peaches cut into ½-inch pieces

TOPPING

1½ cups rolled oats

½ cup chopped pecans

½ cup Kirkland Signature crumbled bacon (optional)

¼ cup brown sugar

½ cup coconut oil or butter (softened)

Preheat oven to 350°F. Coat a 13-by-9-inch baking dish with cooking spray.

Combine baking mix, agave nectar and milk in a bowl. Stir in chopped grapes and peaches until blended. Spread the mixture in the prepared baking dish.

Prepare the topping: In a bowl, combine all ingredients and blend until crumbly and the oil or butter is well distributed. Spread the topping over the fruit batter.

Bake for about 45 minutes, or until a toothpick inserted in the center comes out clean. Makes 6-8 servings.

Recipe developed by Christine W. Jackson, food stylist.

Appetizers & Beverages

Pesto Pizza Caprese
Kirkland Signature

**Cornmeal and flour,
for dusting**

**8 ounces whole-wheat
pizza dough**

**¼ cup Kirkland Signature
Pesto Sauce**

**2 tablespoons shaved
Parmesan cheese, divided**

**1 tablespoon diced
sun-dried tomatoes**

**3 ounces fresh part-skim
mozzarella, sliced**

6 cherry tomatoes, sliced

**2 teaspoons pine nuts,
toasted**

**2 fresh basil leaves,
thinly slivered**

Preheat oven to 425-450°F. Line a sheet pan with parchment paper and lightly dust with cornmeal.

Using a rolling pin and flour for dusting, roll out pizza dough to about ⅛- to ¼-inch thickness and 7-8 inches in diameter. Place on the prepared pan.

Spread pesto sauce evenly over the crust, leaving a ½-inch border. Sprinkle with half of the Parmesan. Sprinkle with sun-dried tomatoes. Add mozzarella and remaining Parmesan, slightly covering the sun-dried tomatoes. Add cherry tomatoes.

Bake for 10-14 minutes, rotating 180 degrees halfway through for even baking. Let cool for 3-5 minutes.

Garnish with toasted pine nuts and basil. Makes 5-6 servings.

Mango and Bacon Barbecue Pizza
Freska Produce

**1 7-inch unbaked
pizza crust**

**2 tablespoons
barbecue sauce**

**½ cup shredded Italian-
blend cheese**

**2 bacon strips, cooked crisp
and coarsely crumbled**

**1 tablespoon sliced green
onion tops**

**1 Freska mango, peeled,
pitted and diced**

Preheat oven to 450°F.

Place pizza crust on a large baking sheet. Spread with barbecue sauce, then sprinkle with cheese, bacon, green onions and mango.

Bake for 8-10 minutes, or until lightly browned around the edges. Let cool slightly, then cut into small wedges. Makes 2-3 servings (or serves 1 as an entrée).

Roasted Garlic Pizzettas

Panné Provincio

1 Panné Provincio roasted garlic batard loaf

2 red bell peppers, divided

1 eggplant

1 zucchini

2 yellow squash

¼ cup olive oil

1 tablespoon salt

1 teaspoon ground black pepper

2 ounces shredded Parmesan cheese

8 fresh basil leaves, chopped

SAUCE

1 garlic clove, minced

1 teaspoon minced fresh thyme

1 teaspoon olive oil

1 teaspoon champagne vinegar

1 tablespoon heavy whipping cream

¼ teaspoon salt

GOAT CHEESE SPREAD

6 ounces goat cheese

1 tablespoon minced fresh thyme

½ teaspoon minced fresh rosemary

½ teaspoon ground black pepper

Preheat the grill to medium. Slice the bread on the bias into ¼-inch-thick slices. Grill for 1 minute on each side.

Grill bell peppers until blackened. Place in a bowl and cover. After 15 minutes, remove blackened skin and seeds. Slice 1 pepper into ¼-inch strips. Reserve the second pepper for the sauce.

Cut eggplant, zucchini and squash into ¼-inch slices. Lightly coat with olive oil and season with salt and pepper. Grill for 2 minutes per side.

Prepare the sauce: Sauté garlic and thyme in oil over medium-low heat until soft. Transfer to a blender and add the second grilled bell pepper, vinegar, cream and salt. Blend until smooth.

Prepare the spread: Blend all ingredients with a spatula.

Spread each crostini with 1 tablespoon of the spread. Layer with 1 eggplant slice, 2 slices of squash and zucchini, and 2 pepper strips. Drizzle with sauce and sprinkle with Parmesan and basil. Makes 6 servings.

Parmesan-Encrusted Spinach & Cheese Ravioli
Monterey Gourmet Foods

1 pound fresh Monterey Gourmet Foods Spinach & Cheese Ravioli

¾ cup extra-virgin olive oil, plus more for coating

1 cup all-purpose flour seasoned with salt and pepper to taste

2 large eggs

3 tablespoons water

½ cup grated Parmesan cheese, plus more for garnish

½ cup dry Italian bread crumbs

Your favorite marinara sauce, for serving

Cook ravioli according to package directions. Drain and cool by running under cold water. Let dry. Coat the ravioli lightly with oil.

Place seasoned flour in a shallow dish. Whisk eggs and water in another shallow dish. Combine Parmesan and bread crumbs in another.

Dredge the ravioli in the flour, dip in the egg wash, and then firmly coat with bread crumbs. To help set the breading, freeze for an hour (optional).

In a cast-iron skillet or saucepan, heat ¾ cup oil to 375°F, using a frying thermometer.

Pan-fry the ravioli, placing dome-side down first. Cook for 3-4 minutes on each side, or until golden. Drain on paper towels and keep warm until ready to serve.

Serve with marinara sauce and garnish with Parmesan. Makes 5-6 servings.

Garlic Artichoke Crisps
Christopher Ranch

3 tablespoons extra-virgin olive oil

4 cloves Christopher Ranch Monviso garlic, finely minced

3 cups marinated artichoke hearts, drained and coarsely chopped

2 tomatoes, seeded and diced

1½ cups (12 ounces) cream cheese

12-48 sourdough crisps or crostini

Salt and pepper

Parmesan cheese, shaved

Heat oil in a sauté pan over medium-low heat. Add garlic and cook until tender, about 1½ minutes (do not burn). Add artichokes and tomatoes, stir to blend and turn off the heat.

Spread cream cheese on crisps. Add salt and pepper if desired.

Top each crisp with a spoonful of the artichoke mixture, then Parmesan shavings. Makes 12 servings.

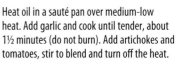

Grape and Goat Cheese Crostini

Anthony Vineyards

1 French baguette

Extra-virgin olive oil

Freshly cracked black pepper

Small bunch of fresh rosemary and parsley

8 ounces fresh soft goat cheese (see note)

1½ pounds assorted red and green seedless grapes

Preheat oven to 375°F.

Holding the knife at a slight diagonal, cut sixteen ⅓- to ½-inch-thick slices from the baguette. Brush the top of each slice with a generous amount of oil and sprinkle with pepper to taste. Arrange on a rimmed baking sheet.

Bake until beginning to brown, about 10 minutes. Remove from the oven and let cool on the sheet for at least 15 minutes.

Chop rosemary and parsley. Mix into goat cheese to taste.

Spread the cheese on the crostini. Cut about 50 small grapes in half; scatter on the crostini.

Arrange the crostini on a platter. Surround with the remaining grape clusters. Makes 8 servings.

Note: Instead of making your own, you can buy herbed goat cheese.

ANTHONY
VINEYARDS

Prosciutto-Wrapped Pears with Parmigiano-Reggiano

Kirkland Signature/Arthur Schuman/Citterio

4 pears

1 12-ounce package Citterio Prosciutto di Parma

6-8 ounces Kirkland Signature Parmigiano-Reggiano cheese

Extra-virgin olive oil

Balsamic vinegar

Juice of 1 lemon

Chives, for garnish (optional)

Cut pears lengthwise into quarters and remove the seeds.

Wrap each pear quarter with 1 piece of prosciutto.

Arrange 4 prosciutto-wrapped pear quarters on each plate.

With a vegetable peeler, shave long shards of Parmigiano-Reggiano and arrange around the pears. Drizzle with oil, vinegar and lemon juice. Garnish with chives. Makes 4 servings.

Blackberry Blueberry Mango Skewers with Cinnamon Cream

Alpine Fresh

Recipe developed by Devin Alexander

Celebrity chef Devin Alexander is the host of Great American Chefs Tour *and author of the* New York Times *best-selling* Biggest Loser Cookbook *series. Visit www.devinalexander.com for more info.*

- 20 6-inch wooden or decorative skewers
- 40 1-inch cubes of Alpine Fresh mango
- 40 Alpine Fresh blackberries
- 40 Alpine Fresh blueberries
- ¼ teaspoon vanilla extract
- ⅛ teaspoon ground cinnamon
- 1 6-ounce container low-fat or fat-free vanilla yogurt

Skewer 1 mango cube, then 1 blackberry and 1 blueberry, then a second mango cube, blackberry and blueberry on each skewer. Arrange the skewers decoratively on a platter. Cover with plastic wrap and refrigerate.

Stir vanilla and cinnamon into the yogurt until well combined. Transfer to a small dipping bowl. Serve immediately with the skewers, or cover and refrigerate until ready to serve. Makes 20 skewers with dip.

Bacon-Wrapped Green Bean Bundles

Alpine Fresh

- Olive oil spray (propellant free)
- 36 Alpine Fresh green beans, trimmed
- 1 teaspoon extra-virgin olive oil
- ¼ teaspoon freshly ground black pepper, or more to taste
- 6 slices 94% fat-free or leaner nitrate-free turkey bacon, cut in half crosswise
- Toothpicks (optional)

Preheat oven to 400°F. Line a small baking sheet with nonstick foil. Lightly mist the foil with olive oil spray.

In a small glass or plastic mixing bowl, toss green beans with oil and pepper.

Place a strip of bacon vertically on a cutting board. Lay 3 green beans horizontally across the end of the bacon closest to you. Roll the bacon tightly around the beans until you reach the opposite end of the bacon. Secure with a toothpick, if necessary, and place on the prepared baking sheet. Repeat with the remaining bacon and beans.

Bake for 8-10 minutes, or until the beans are crisp-tender and the bacon is lightly browned. Makes 4 (3-bundle) servings.

Nutritional information: Each serving has 79 calories, 10 g protein, 4 g carbohydrates, 3 g fat, trace saturated fat, 38 mg cholesterol, 2 g fiber, 300 mg sodium, 2 g sugar.

FRANCE FREEMAN

DALE HOLLINGSWORTH
Costco Produce Buyer

We all know that fruits are a great snack, an easy addition to salads, and make for mouthwatering desserts. Now it's time to think about incorporating them into appetizers. With this triple-fruit recipe, you'll be getting a nutrient-dense tasty treat that's packed with vitamins A, C, E and a B complex plus potassium, magnesium, fiber and folic acid.

While I've always thought that French beans are a near-perfect side dish, it's their versatility that proves they are a great grocery item. They are excellent additions to stir-fries, soups, salads and casseroles, and couldn't be easier to pickle. Eating French beans is an easy way to increase your daily intake of vitamin A, B_{12}, B_6 and C while consuming few calories. They also contain an abundance of antioxidants, which helps boost immunity. With healthy and delicious appetizers like these, who cares if you have room for dinner?

I hope these recipes will encourage you to find different ways to use these products as you explore new dishes to prepare for family and friends.

Hawaiian Kalua Pig Tostadas with Tomato Cucumber Salsa

Eurofresh Farms

1½ cups pureed fresh mango

½ cup hoisin sauce

1½ cups Eurofresh Roma tomatoes
cut in small dice

1½ cups Eurofresh English
cucumbers cut in small dice

4 radishes, julienned

1 teaspoon grated fresh ginger

¼ cup Maui onions cut in small dice

2 tablespoons rice wine vinegar

2 teaspoons sesame oil

Salt

2 6-ounce bags taro chips
(about 32 chips)

½ cup crumbled cotija cheese

2 tablespoons sliced green onions

KALUA PIG

4 ti leaves or banana leaves

5 pounds pork shoulder,
cut in ½-inch cubes

2 tablespoons Hawaiian sea salt

2 tablespoons liquid smoke flavoring

Preheat oven to 400°F.

Prepare the pig: Line a roasting pan with half the leaves. Mix remaining ingredients. Place the mixture on the leaves and cover with remaining leaves.

Pour in 1 cup water and cover the pan with a tight lid. Roast for 2 hours. Carefully remove the lid and the top leaves. Let cool to room temperature. Shred the pork with 2 forks. Set aside 2 cups for the recipe and keep warm. Refrigerate the remaining pork for up to 5 days.

In a bowl, combine mango and hoisin sauce. Set aside.

In a large bowl, mix tomatoes, cucumbers, radishes, ginger, Maui onions, vinegar, oil and salt to taste. Set aside.

To assemble, lay taro chips on a platter. Layer with 2 cups pork, mango sauce, tomato cucumber salsa and cheese. Garnish with green onions. Makes 12 servings.

Recipe developed by Matt Alleshouse, chef/partner, Urban Chefs Az.

Holiday Meatballs
New York Style Sausage

1 pound New York Style Italian sausage links, casings removed

1 pound cooked, peeled chestnuts, ground

½ teaspoon salt

1 teaspoon freshly ground pepper

¼ cup freshly grated Parmesan or Romano cheese

1 tablespoon finely chopped fresh parsley

1 tablespoon finely chopped fresh marjoram

1 cup flour, seasoned lightly with salt and pepper

¼ cup extra-virgin olive oil

12 small pearl onions, peeled

1 cup dry white wine

In a bowl, combine sausage, chestnuts, salt, pepper, grated cheese, parsley and marjoram; blend well. Shape into meatballs the size of walnuts and roll in the seasoned flour. In a skillet, heat a thin layer of oil over medium-high heat. Add the meatballs and onions to the skillet and fry until the meatballs are just cooked through, about 10-15 minutes. Drain off excess oil.

Add wine and let it simmer down into a sauce. Cover and cook over low heat for about 5 minutes. Makes 8 servings.

Note: If unable to find chestnuts, use 1 pound mashed potatoes.

Party Meatballs
New York Style Sausage

½ cup red or white wine

½ cup seasoned dry bread crumbs

1 pound New York Style Italian sausage links (hot or mild)

4 tablespoons vegetable oil

1 tablespoon grated Romano cheese

1 tablespoon coarsely chopped fresh Italian parsley

Put wine in a small bowl. Put bread crumbs on a flat plate. Lay out a sheet of waxed paper.

Cut open sausages and remove from the casings. Pinch off enough sausage to make a tiny meatball, about 1 inch in diameter. Dip the meat into the wine and roll firmly into a meatball. The wine prevents it from sticking to your palms. Then roll the meatball in bread crumbs to cover entirely and place on the waxed paper. Repeat the procedure with the remaining sausage. It makes approximately 24 meatballs.

In a nonstick frying pan, preheat oil to medium-high. Place the meatballs in the hot oil and cook, turning when they are dark brown, until they are just cooked through. Watch the heat so that they don't burn. Transfer the finished meatballs to paper towels to absorb excess oil.

Arrange the meatballs on your favorite plate. Garnish with grated Romano and parsley. These meatballs hold well in a food warmer, covered tightly with plastic wrap and foil. Makes 6 servings.

Peanut Chicken Mini Phyllo Cups
J.M. Smucker Co.

1 tablespoon Crisco
Pure Olive Oil

1 pound ground chicken
thigh meat

¼ cup diced red bell pepper

2 tablespoons chopped
green onion

¼ cup Jif Creamy
Peanut Butter

¼ cup water

2 tablespoons soy sauce

1 teaspoon finely
chopped garlic

1 teaspoon finely chopped
fresh ginger

⅛ teaspoon ground
black pepper

2 tablespoons fresh
lime juice

3 15-count packages
frozen prebaked mini
phyllo shells, thawed

2 tablespoons chopped
fresh cilantro

Heat oil in a large skillet over medium heat. Add chicken and cook until crumbly and no longer pink. Add bell pepper and green onion. Cook for 1 minute. Drain.

In a small saucepan, combine peanut butter, water, soy sauce, garlic, ginger and black pepper. Cook over low heat, stirring until smooth. Stir in lime juice.

Pour the sauce over the cooked chicken and stir until thoroughly combined. Fill each phyllo shell with 1 tablespoon of the chicken mixture. Garnish with cilantro. Makes 45 servings.

Nancy's Lighthouse Point Langostino Lobster Tail Sliders
Camanchaca

1 pound Kirkland Signature
frozen fully cooked
Langostino Lobster Tails

½ cup mayonnaise

½ cup finely chopped sweet
onion (1 medium onion)

½ cup finely chopped
celery (2 large stalks)

¼ teaspoon Old Bay
seasoning

¼ teaspoon salt

½ teaspoon cracked pepper

4 Kirkland Signature
fresh-baked rolls

4 tablespoons unsalted
butter, softened

4 lettuce leaves,
washed and dried

Parsley sprigs, for garnish

Thaw langostino lobster tails under cold running water for a couple of minutes and drain well. Pat dry.

In a bowl, mix the thawed langostino lobster tails, mayonnaise, onion, celery, seasoning, salt and pepper.

Slice rolls in half and spread with butter.

Heat a skillet over medium heat. Add the buttered buns to the pan, cut side down, and cook until they are toasted to your preference, about 1 minute.

Place a lettuce leaf on each bun and top with the langostino lobster tail mixture. Garnish with parsley sprigs.

If desired, serve with your favorite salad or chips. Makes 4 servings.

Clams Casino
Cedar Key Aquaculture Farms

½ cup fresh bread crumbs

4 tablespoons butter, softened

2 tablespoons finely chopped red bell pepper

2 tablespoons finely chopped fresh parsley

1 tablespoon finely chopped green onion

½ teaspoon cayenne pepper

24 Cedar Key Sweets farm-raised clams

6 bacon slices, cooked crisp and crumbled

Preheat the broiler.

In a bowl, combine bread crumbs, butter, bell pepper, parsley, green onion and cayenne pepper. Blend well.

Shuck clams, leaving loosened clam meat in one half of each shell; discard the other half.

Place the clams on the half shell in a baking dish. Cover each with about 1 teaspoon of the bread-crumb mixture.

Broil the clams 4-6 inches from the heat for 3-4 minutes, or until browned and the clams are just cooked through.

Garnish with bacon and serve immediately. Makes 4 servings.

Clams in Pesto Broth
Taylor Shellfish Farms

2½ pounds Manila clams

2 tablespoons unsalted butter

2 tablespoons olive oil

½ cup chopped onions

¼ cup dry white wine

¼ cup prepared basil pesto, or to taste

¼ cup clam juice

Crusty bread, for serving

Rinse clams well in cold water and drain. Discard any clams with broken shells.

In a large deep skillet or wok, melt butter and oil over medium-high heat. Add onions and sauté until translucent.

Add the drained clams and toss with the onions. Add wine and toss to blend.

Cover tightly and cook until the clams are just starting to open, about 5-8 minutes. Add pesto and clam juice; toss the mixture. Cover and continue cooking until all the clams have opened. Discard any clams that do not open.

Serve in bowls with the sauce and warm crusty bread for dipping. Makes 2-4 servings.

Note: This recipe works best with small batches of clams prepared in a large skillet.

Steamed Mussels in Green Curry Sauce
North Coast Seafoods

3 tablespoons vegetable oil

1 cup onion cut in small dice

1 tablespoon chopped garlic

3 tablespoons Maesri green curry paste

1 cup coconut milk

2 pounds North Coast Seafoods PEI mussels

1 tablespoon chopped fresh parsley

1 tablespoon chopped fresh basil

Salt and pepper

4 naans (Indian flatbreads) or crusty bread

Fresh basil leaves, for garnish

Heat oil over medium heat in a pot large enough to hold the mussels. Add onion and garlic; sauté until the onion is soft, about 3-4 minutes.

Add curry paste and coconut milk, and stir until everything is combined.

Turn the heat up to high. Add mussels, cover the pot and cook for 3-4 minutes. When the mussels have opened, turn off the heat. Add parsley and basil. Season to taste with salt and pepper.

Serve in bowls with naan and garnish with basil leaves. Makes 4 servings.

Tip: This dish will serve 2 as an entrée.

Impossibly Easy Mini Crab Cake Pies
General Mills

2 6-ounce cans crabmeat, drained, flaked

½ teaspoon seafood seasoning

1 tablespoon oil

½ cup chopped onion

½ cup chopped red bell pepper

½ cup chopped green bell pepper

1 cup shredded mozzarella cheese

½ cup Original Bisquick mix

½ cup milk

2 eggs

AIOLI

½ cup mayonnaise

½ teaspoon seafood seasoning

1 tablespoon fresh lemon juice

Preheat oven to 375°F. Coat 12 regular-size muffin cups with cooking spray.

In a bowl, mix crabmeat and seafood seasoning; set aside.

In a 10-inch skillet, heat oil over medium-high heat. Add vegetables and cook for 4 minutes. Add the crab and heat through. Let cool for 5 minutes, then stir in cheese.

In a bowl, whisk Bisquick, milk and eggs. Spoon 1 tablespoonful into each muffin cup. Top with ¼ cup crab mixture. Spoon 1 tablespoon baking mixture on top.

Bake for 30 minutes, or until golden brown. Cool 5 minutes. With a knife, remove the pies from the pan and cool on a rack for 10 minutes.

Prepare the aioli: In a bowl, mix all ingredients. Top the pies with aioli. Makes 6 servings.

Black Bean and Corn Salsa
S&W Beans

1 15-ounce can S&W black beans, drained and rinsed

1 15-ounce can whole-kernel corn, drained

1 14.5-ounce can diced tomatoes with jalapeños, drained

½ cup sliced green onions

2 tablespoons olive oil

½ teaspoon ground cumin

¼ cup chopped fresh cilantro

1 tablespoon lime juice

Combine all ingredients in a medium bowl and toss.

Serve with warmed tortilla chips.

Makes about 8 servings.

Rosarita Margarita Dip
ConAgra Foods

1 10-ounce can Ro*Tel Original Diced Tomatoes & Green Chilies, drained, divided

1 16-ounce can Rosarita Traditional Refried Beans

2 cups prepared guacamole

1 cup (4 ounces) shredded Cheddar cheese

¼ cup sliced green onions

½ cup sour cream

¼ cup sliced ripe olives

Tortilla chips, for serving (optional)

Reserve ½ cup of the drained tomatoes; set aside. Combine the remaining drained tomatoes and beans in a medium bowl; mix well. Spoon the mixture evenly into four 8- to 9-ounce margarita glasses.

Divide guacamole, cheese, reserved tomatoes, green onions, sour cream and olives equally in layers over the beans in the glasses.

Insert 1 tortilla chip into the dip in each glass for garnish. Serve with additional tortilla chips, if desired. Makes 4-8 servings.

Note: Martini glasses (4 ounces) can be used for smaller portions.

Tequila Guacamole
Avocados from Mexico

¼ cup pickled jalapeños, finely chopped

¼ cup vinegar from the pickled jalapeños

½ cup pickled carrots, finely chopped

⅓ cup finely chopped white onion

Juice of ½ lime (1 tablespoon)

Dried oregano to taste

¼ cup tequila of your choice

4 fully ripened avocados from Mexico, halved, pitted and peeled

1 tablespoon olive oil

Salt

Chips, for serving

In a bowl, combine jalapeños, jalapeño vinegar, carrots, onion, lime juice, oregano and tequila. Let marinate for 2 minutes.

Coarsely mash avocados with a fork. Add to the jalapeño mixture. Stir in oil and salt to taste.

Serve with chips or on tostadas or tacos. Makes 8 servings.

Crema de Bocado (Cream Cheese Bacon Avocado Dip)

Don Miguel Mexican Foods

3 ripe avocados
¾ cup whipped cream cheese
1 cup bacon bits (pieces)

2 teaspoons garlic powder
1 teaspoon onion powder
Salt and pepper (optional)

Cut avocados in half, remove the pits and scoop out the flesh into a bowl. Gently mash with a fork.

Mix in cream cheese, bacon bits, garlic powder and onion powder. Add salt and/or pepper to taste.

Serve with Don Miguel Chicken & Cheese Mini Tacos for an amazing appetizer. Makes 6 servings.

Pepper Quesadillas
Windset Farms

8 flour tortillas

3 Dolce Super Sweet baby bell peppers, seeded and sliced

½ Gusto hot pepper, seeded and finely chopped

3 green onions, thinly sliced

2 cups shredded Monterey Jack cheese

CONCERTO TOMATO SALSA

1½ pounds Concerto grape tomatoes

2 garlic cloves, finely chopped

½ medium red onion, finely chopped

3 Dolce Super Sweet baby bell peppers, seeded and chopped

¼ cup chopped fresh cilantro

½ teaspoon ground cumin

1 teaspoon kosher salt

Prepare the salsa: Place all the ingredients in a food processor and pulse to blend.

Place 4 tortillas on a work surface. Dividing evenly, scatter sweet and hot peppers and green onions over each, leaving a ½-inch border all around. Sprinkle ½ cup cheese over each. Top with the remaining tortillas. Press lightly to seal.

Place 1 quesadilla on a paper towel. Top with another paper towel, a quesadilla and a third paper towel. Microwave the 2 stacked quesadillas on high for 2 minutes, or until the cheese has melted. Carefully separate (they will be very hot) and remove the paper towels. Place the quesadillas on a platter. Repeat with the remaining 2 quesadillas.

Cut each quesadilla into 4 wedges and serve with the salsa. Makes 4 servings.

Recipe developed by chef Dana Reinhardt.

Tuna Avocado Dip
Chicken of the Sea

1 7-ounce can Chicken of the Sea solid white tuna in water, drained

1 large ripe avocado, peeled and mashed

1 tablespoon freshly squeezed lemon juice

1 garlic clove, minced

2 teaspoons freshly minced onion

4 drops hot pepper sauce

Crackers or fresh cut vegetables, for serving (optional)

In a medium bowl, flake tuna. Mix in avocado, lemon juice, garlic, onion and hot sauce.

Serve with crackers or fresh cut vegetables, or use as a sandwich filling. Makes 6 appetizer servings (or 2 sandwiches).

Carrot Hummus
Grimmway Farms

1 pound Bunny-Luv organic baby carrots

1 15-ounce can chickpeas, drained

½ cup lemon juice, from about 2 lemons

¼ cup water

¼ cup tahini

2 garlic cloves

½ teaspoon salt

½ teaspoon ground cumin

Place all ingredients in a food processor and pulse several times to coarsely chop. Then let the food processor run for about 2 minutes, or until the hummus is smooth.

Using a spatula, transfer the hummus to a serving bowl.

Serve with baby carrots, red bell peppers, celery or pita chips. Makes 6-8 servings.

Hummus Dip
Kirkland Signature

1 15-ounce can garbanzo beans or chickpeas, liquid drained and reserved

1 garlic clove, peeled

2 teaspoons ground cumin

½ teaspoon sea salt

1 tablespoon extra-virgin olive oil (optional)

Kirkland Signature chips, for serving

In a blender or food processor, combine garbanzo beans, garlic, cumin, salt and oil. Blend until pureed.

At low speed, gradually add the bean liquid until the hummus has the desired consistency.

Serve with chips. Makes 4 servings.

Variations: Add ½ cup roasted red peppers. Or add ½ cup sun-dried tomatoes marinated in olive oil (omit the 1 tablespoon olive oil).

Mango Smoothie
Profood

1 cup Philippine Brand dried mango

1 banana

½ cup yogurt

1 cup 100% pure mango juice

6 ice cubes

Reconstitute dried mango by soaking in warm water for about 10 minutes, or until soft. Cut into smaller pieces.

In a blender, combine banana, yogurt and mango juice; blend until well mixed. Add the reconstituted mangoes and ice cubes, and blend until smooth. Makes 1-2 servings.

Golden Crush
Sunkist Growers

3 bananas, sliced

1 cup sugar

1 cup milk

½ cup freshly squeezed Sunkist orange juice

¼ cup freshly squeezed Sunkist lemon juice

4-5 cups lemon/lime-flavored soda

4-5 cups freshly squeezed Sunkist orange juice (12-15 oranges)

Garnish: orange cartwheel slices and maraschino cherries threaded on short wooden skewers

In a blender, combine bananas, sugar, milk, ½ cup orange juice and lemon juice. Blend until smooth. Pour into 2-3 ice cube trays. Freeze.

To serve, place 3-4 frozen cubes in each glass. Let stand at room temperature for 5 minutes. Pour ½ cup soda and ½ cup orange juice over the cubes in each glass and stir. Garnish with an orange slice and cherry on a skewer. Makes 8 servings.

Sunkist

Cranberry Cocktail Lemonade

Kirkland Signature/Cott/Dream Foods

16 ounces Italian Volcano lemon juice

16 ounces Kirkland Signature cranberry juice cocktail

4 ounces agave nectar

32 ounces club soda

8 ounces vodka (optional)

Crushed ice, for serving

Mint leaves, for garnish

Stir together lemon juice, cranberry juice and agave nectar until dissolved. Add club soda. For a refreshing cocktail, also add vodka.

Pour over crushed ice. Garnish with mint if desired. Makes 8 servings.

Note: This is a great-looking beverage to serve at a party.

Skinny Coco-Açaí Lemonade
Vita Coco

2 lemon wedges

1¼ ounces VeeV Açaí Spirit (see note)

1 tablespoon agave nectar

4 ounces Vita Coco pure coconut water

Splash of sparkling lemonade or club soda (optional)

Sprig of mint or basil and a lemon wedge, for garnish (optional)

Fill a cocktail shaker with ice.

Squeeze lemon wedges into the shaker. Add VeeV Açaí Spirit, agave nectar and coconut water. Shake well.

Strain into an ice-filled rocks glass and top with sparkling lemonade. Garnish with a mint sprig and lemon wedge. Just 110 calories! Makes 1 serving.

Note: This can also be served as a mocktail—just skip the VeeV.

Minty Lime Cooler
Paramount Citrus

3 tablespoons grated lime zest (see note)

8 large sprigs fresh mint

2 cups sugar

2 cups water

1½ cups fresh-squeezed Paramount Citrus lime juice

3 cups water (or soda water)

Lime wheels and fresh mint sprigs, for garnish

Combine lime zest, mint, sugar and 2 cups water in a saucepan. Bring to a boil over high heat, cook for 1 minute, then remove from the heat. Let sit for 30 minutes to steep.

Discard the mint from the syrup. In a large pitcher, combine the syrup, lime juice and 3 cups water.

Serve over ice in tall glasses garnished with lime wheels and mint sprigs. Keep refrigerated for up to 1 week. Makes 8-10 servings.

Note: Zest is the outer peel of the fruit—with no white pith attached. You can remove the zest from the fruit with a fine zesting tool that makes long, pretty strands, or you can peel off the zest with an ordinary potato peeler, being careful not to get any white pith, and then finely mince it.

Recipe developed by Kathy Casey Food Studios for Paramount Citrus.

PARAMOUNT
Citrus

Green Tea Peach Virgin Sangria
Kirkland Signature/Ito En

**5 Kirkland Signature/
Ito En green tea bags**

3 cups peach nectar

½ cup honey

16 mint leaves

2 kiwis, peeled and sliced

1 peach, peeled and diced

1 apple, peeled and diced

1 lime, sliced, for garnish

Steep tea bags in 5 cups of hot water (176°F) for 30-40 seconds. Remove the tea bags. Let the tea cool, then refrigerate.

When the green tea is chilled, pour into a pitcher and add peach nectar, honey and mint leaves. Stir well, muddling the mint leaves. Add the fruits, along with several ice cubes.

Serve in glasses garnished with a lime slice. Makes 8 servings.

Summer Peach Sangria
Fowler Packing

**1 bottle (750 ml) dry
white wine**

¾ cup peach schnapps

1 cup club soda

¼ cup agave nectar

3 peaches, sliced

**¾ cup green
seedless grapes**

**¾ cup red
seedless grapes**

Stir together wine, schnapps, club soda and agave nectar.

Add fruit and chill for 2 hours.

Serve chilled over ice. Makes 6 servings.

Blueberry Mojito

Naturipe

8 fresh Naturipe blueberries,
  plus more for garnish

6 fresh mint leaves,
  plus more for garnish

3 ounces club soda

2 ounces lemon-
  flavored rum

1 tablespoon simple syrup
  (see note)

1 lime wedge

Muddle blueberries and mint with a splash of soda in a cocktail shaker until they're crushed.

Fill the shaker with ice, then add rum, simple syrup and lime.

Shake together, then strain into a glass filled with ice. Add the remaining soda.

Garnish with more mint and blueberries. Makes 1 serving.

Note: This recipe makes a refreshing drink without alcohol. You can make simple syrup by combining 2 cups sugar with 2 cups water. Bring to a quick boil. Let cool, then store, covered, in the refrigerator for up to 1 month.

Ruby Red Florida Grapefruit Margarita

Greene River Marketing

5 Ruby Red grapefruit

Kosher salt or any other
  coarse salt

7 ounces tequila

⅓ cup vodka or
  Ruby Red vodka

¼ cup freshly squeezed
  lime juice

¼ cup simple syrup
  (see note)

6-8 ice cubes

8-10 slices fresh grapefruit

Use 1-2 wedges of grapefruit to rub the rims of 8 glasses. Dip the rims into the salt to coat each glass. Set aside.

Juice the remaining grapefruit, to yield 2 cups.

Place the grapefruit juice, tequila, vodka, lime juice, simple syrup and ice in a blender and blend until smooth. Pour into the glasses and garnish with grapefruit slices. Makes 8 servings.

Note: You can make simple syrup by combining 2 cups sugar with 2 cups water. Bring to a quick boil. Let cool, then store, covered, in the refrigerator for up to 1 month.

Soups & Sides

Broccoli Cheese Soup
Eat Smart

4 tablespoons butter
1 small yellow onion, diced
2 garlic cloves, minced
28 ounces Eat Smart broccoli florets, chopped into very small pieces
4 14.5-ounce cans low-sodium chicken broth
2 teaspoons garlic powder
1 teaspoon salt
½ teaspoon ground pepper
1 1-pound processed cheese loaf, cut into small cubes
2 cups half-and-half
⅔ cup cornstarch
1 cup cold water

In a large stockpot, melt butter over medium heat. Add onion and garlic; sauté until softened.

Stir in broccoli and chicken broth. Add garlic powder, salt and pepper. Simmer until the broccoli is tender, about 10-15 minutes.

Reduce the heat and add cheese cubes, stirring until melted.

Mix in half-and-half.

In a small bowl, stir cornstarch into the water until dissolved. Stir into the soup and cook, stirring continuously to prevent sticking, until it thickens. Makes 12 servings.

Tip: To reduce the calories, substitute milk for the half-and-half and use reduced-fat cheese.

Variation: Add 2 baked potatoes, cut into bite-size cubes, when you add the cheese and garnish with cooked diced bacon. For extra spice, add your favorite hot sauce.

Asparagus and Brie Soup
Jacobs Malcolm & Burtt/Gourmet Trading/ NewStar Fresh Foods

½ pound asparagus
1 tablespoon salt
⅓ cup butter
¼ cup flour
3 cups chicken broth
½ cup sweet white wine
1 cup heavy cream
½ cup Brie, rind removed and cut into chunks

Snap or cut off the white portion at the bottom of each asparagus spear and discard. Cut the asparagus into 2-inch pieces.

Fill a large pot half full of water, add salt and bring to a boil. Add the asparagus to the boiling water and cook for 3 minutes. Drain and immediately plunge into a bowl of ice water. Drain.

In a saucepan, heat butter over medium-high heat. Add the asparagus and sauté until tender. Stir in flour, reduce the heat and cook for 2 minutes.

Stir in broth, wine and cream. Bring to a boil, then reduce the heat and simmer for 10 minutes.

Transfer the soup to a blender or processor and puree. Return to the pot and reheat to a simmer. Stir in cheese and continue to simmer for 5 minutes, or until the cheese has melted. Makes 4 servings.

JACOBS MALCOLM & BURTT

Potato and Onion Cheddar Soup

Basin Gold Cooperative

1 tablespoon unsalted butter

2 Basin Gold jumbo yellow onions, coarsely chopped

2 pounds large Basin Gold russet potatoes, peeled and chopped into ½-inch cubes

1½ teaspoons minced garlic

6 cups chicken stock (healthy option: low-sodium broth)

½ teaspoon dry mustard

2 cups heavy cream (healthy option: nonfat half-and-half)

2 cups extra-sharp or smoked Cheddar cheese (healthy option: 2% milk sharp Cheddar)

½ teaspoon hot pepper sauce

2 dashes Worcestershire sauce

½ teaspoon salt

½ teaspoon freshly ground pepper

3 tablespoons chopped chives, for garnish

2 tablespoons bacon bits, for garnish

In a medium saucepan, melt butter over moderate heat. Add onions, potatoes and garlic; cook, stirring occasionally, until the onions are translucent (about 10 minutes)—do not let the onions brown.

Add chicken stock and bring to a boil over high heat, then reduce the heat and simmer until the potatoes are tender (about 12 minutes).

Working in batches, puree the soup in a food processor or blender.

In a large saucepan, whisk dry mustard into cream. Bring to a boil over high heat, then reduce to moderate heat and simmer for 3 minutes. Stir in the pureed soup and simmer, stirring occasionally, for 4 minutes. (Up to this stage, the soup can be made up to 2 days ahead of time. Refrigerate in an airtight container and reheat before continuing.)

Stir in grated cheese until just melted. Season with hot sauce, Worcestershire sauce, salt and pepper.

Sprinkle with chives and bacon bits, and serve. Makes 6-8 servings.

Basin Gold

Icy Fruit Gazpacho with Spicy Grilled Shrimp
Dole

2 cups vegetable juice

2 large tomatoes, coarsely chopped

1 20-ounce can Dole Tropical Gold pineapple chunks, drained, divided

1½ cups Dole frozen mango chunks, partially thawed, divided

1 tablespoon honey

1 teaspoon chili garlic sauce

¼ cup chopped fresh mint leaves

1 cup orange juice

1 pound medium-large raw shrimp, peeled and deveined

1-2 tablespoons dry Creole seasoning

Mint sprigs (optional)

In a blender or food processor, combine vegetable juice, tomatoes, 1 cup *each* pineapple and mango chunks, honey and chili garlic sauce. Cover and blend until smooth.

Add the remaining pineapple and mango chunks and mint. Pulse 2-3 times just to chop the fruit.

Pour into a large bowl and stir in orange juice. Chill for at least 1 hour.

Preheat the grill to medium-high.

In a large bowl, toss shrimp with Creole seasoning to coat well. Grill for 3-4 minutes or until pink, turning once.

Serve the chilled gazpacho in shallow bowls. Top with the shrimp. Garnish with mint sprigs, if desired. Makes 6 servings.

Bicolor Sweet Mini Pepper Soup
Royal Flavor

1 2-pound bag Royal Flavor sweet mini peppers

½ onion, chopped

2 Roma tomatoes, chopped

2 celery stalks, chopped

2 cups water

2 cups milk

½ pound goat cheese, crumbled

2 ounces butter

½ pound Gouda cheese, grated

Salt and pepper

You will be making two separate soups. Use all of the red peppers and half of the yellow and orange peppers. Stem, seed and chop the peppers.

Prepare the first soup: In a saucepan, combine red peppers and half of the onion, tomatoes and celery. Add half of the water and bring to a rolling boil, then remove from the heat and let cool. Puree in a blender, then strain. Return to the stove and bring to a boil. Add half of the milk and goat cheese. Once the cheese has melted, reduce the heat and add half of the butter and Gouda cheese. Season to taste with salt and pepper. Let stand for 2 minutes before serving.

Repeat the process for the second soup, using yellow and orange peppers.

To serve, pour equal parts of both soups into each serving bowl. Makes 6-8 servings.

Three-Bean Chili with Salmon Burgers

Trident Seafoods

2 cups chopped onion
  (1 medium onion)

2 garlic cloves, minced

1 tablespoon olive oil

1 15-ounce can garbanzo
  beans, drained

1 15-ounce can butter
  beans, drained

1 15-ounce can white or red
  kidney beans, drained

2 cups chicken broth

1½ cups chopped, seeded fresh
  green chile (1 large Anaheim
  or poblano chile)

4 teaspoons dried crushed
  Italian seasoning

2 teaspoons ground cumin

1 teaspoon ground coriander

½ teaspoon salt

½ teaspoon ground black pepper

⅛-¼ teaspoon smoked
  paprika (optional)

3 Trident Seafoods frozen
  salmon burgers

In a large saucepan, combine onion, garlic and oil; sauté over medium-high heat until the onion is tender.

Stir in beans, chicken broth, chile and seasonings. Bring to a boil, then reduce the heat and simmer for 15-20 minutes, or until slightly thickened.

Meanwhile, cook salmon burgers according to package directions. Break into bite-size pieces and stir into the bean mixture. Cook for 2 minutes, or until all ingredients are heated through.

Serve hot and garnish with optional condiments such as green salsa, sour cream or freshly chopped cilantro or tomatoes. Makes 4-5 servings (about 5 cups).

CHARLES H. BUNDRANT
Founder & Chairman

JOE BUNDRANT
Executive Vice President

Trident's Wild Salmon Burgers, featured here, are prime examples of the care we take to harvest the freshest wild salmon and create delicious, healthy and convenient products that are simple to prepare right out of the freezer— whether pan-fried, grilled on the barbecue or baked in the oven. Remarkably versatile, they deliver great flavor in a traditional burger bun or a toasted English muffin—and you'll be amazed how they perform in this delicious homemade Three-Bean Chili.

With our convenient resealable package, you cook only what you need. There's no easier way to put healthy, wild salmon on the table. We're certain our featured recipe will delight your family and your guests, and we hope it will spark your imagination to incorporate wild salmon into a new family favorite of your own.

Sweet Hot Chili
Kirkland Signature/Bolthouse Farms

1 28-ounce can
   crushed tomatoes

2 cups Kirkland Signature
   100% Organic Carrot Juice

1 15- to 16-ounce can
   chili beans

1 15-ounce can
   red kidney beans

Jalapeño, diced, to taste

1½ tablespoons chili powder

1½ tablespoons
   ground cumin

1 tablespoon fresh thyme

1¼ pounds ground turkey

5 ounces pork chorizo

3 garlic cloves, diced

1 green bell pepper, diced

1 medium onion, diced

Sour cream and fresh
   cilantro, for serving
   (optional)

In a large pot, combine tomatoes, carrot juice, chili beans, kidney beans, jalapeño, chili powder, cumin and thyme. Bring to a boil, then reduce the heat to low. Cover and cook for 40 minutes.

Meanwhile, in a sauté pan over medium heat, lightly brown turkey, chorizo, garlic, bell pepper and onion. Set aside.

Add the meat mixture to the pot and simmer for another 15 minutes.

To serve, garnish with sour cream and cilantro. Makes 8 servings.

Grill-Roasted Vegetables with Planked Brie
Rupari Foods

Serve as an accompaniment to Tony Roma's ribs.

1 small red onion

1 small white onion

1 large red bell pepper

12 garlic cloves, peeled

4 ounces crimini mushrooms

½ pound small
   carrots, peeled

1 pound mini new potatoes

3 tablespoons olive oil

Fresh thyme, salt and pepper

1 mini Brie cheese wheel
   (approximately 300 g)

SPECIAL EQUIPMENT

1 cedar grilling plank
   (½ inch thick, 8 by 8 inches)

2 aluminum lasagna pans
   (12 by 10 inches)

Soak the plank in water for 1 hour.

Preheat the grill to medium-high (400-500°F).

Cut onions and pepper into 2-inch chunks. In a large bowl, combine garlic, mushrooms and vegetables. Drizzle with oil and season to taste with thyme, salt and pepper. Pour into the pans. Place directly over the grill flame and close the lid. Grill-roast, stirring occasionally, for 45-60 minutes, or until tender, lightly browned and crisp.

Place Brie on the plank. Set on the grill and close the lid. Plank-grill for 12-15 minutes, or until the cheese is hot, slightly bulging and very soft.

Pierce the cheese rind and drizzle molten Brie over the vegetables. Gently toss and serve immediately. Makes 8 servings.

TONY ROMA'S
WORLD · FAMOUS · RIBS

Roasted Brussels Sprouts with Prosciutto and Parmesan
Chairmans Foods

Serve as an accompaniment to Kirkland Signature chicken pot pie.

2 pounds Brussels sprouts, rinsed and trimmed

4 tablespoons olive oil

3 ounces prosciutto, diced

1 large yellow onion, julienned

4 garlic cloves, chopped

Salt and black pepper

¼ cup shredded Parmigiano-Reggiano cheese

Preheat oven to 350°F.

Bring 6 cups water to a boil in a large pot. Boil Brussels sprouts for 3 minutes. Remove with a slotted spoon and place in a colander to drain off excess water.

In an ovenproof sauté pan, heat oil over medium heat. Add prosciutto and cook until slightly crispy. Add onion and sauté until lightly browned. Stir in garlic, Brussels sprouts and a pinch of salt and pepper. Sprinkle Parmigiano-Reggiano over the top.

Transfer the pan to the oven and bake for about 10 minutes, or until the cheese melts.

Makes 6-8 servings.

Savory Stuffed Artichokes
Boskovich Farms

4 Boskovich Farms artichokes

1 lemon, halved

2 cups dry bread crumbs

1 cup freshly grated Parmesan or Romano cheese, divided

⅓ cup chopped flat-leaf parsley leaves

2 teaspoons salt

1 teaspoon ground black pepper

6-8 garlic cloves, finely chopped

Extra-virgin olive oil

Using a serrated knife, cut off the artichoke stems, creating a flat bottom. Cut about 1 inch off the tops. Pull off the tough outermost leaves; trim the leaf tips with kitchen shears. Rub cut areas with lemon. Open the leaves with your thumbs to make room for stuffing.

In a large bowl, combine bread crumbs, ¾ cup cheese, parsley, salt, pepper and garlic.

Drizzle oil over the artichokes. Spoon a generous amount of stuffing into each artichoke, working it in between the leaves.

Place a steamer basket in a large pot; fill the pot with water to just below the basket. Place the stuffed artichokes in the steamer, cover and bring the water to a boil. Steam for 30-40 minutes, or until the leaves are tender.

To serve, drizzle with oil and sprinkle with the remaining cheese. Makes 4 servings.

Grilled Coffeehouse Asparagus
J.M. Smucker Co.

1 pound fresh asparagus, trimmed

1 tablespoon Crisco Pure Canola Oil

3 tablespoons balsamic vinegar

3 tablespoons reduced-sodium soy sauce

1 tablespoon sugar

2 teaspoons Folgers Classic Instant Coffee Crystals

Heat a grill grate or grill pan over medium-high heat.

Brush asparagus with oil. Grill for 3 minutes. Turn and grill for an additional 3-4 minutes.

In a small saucepan, stir together balsamic vinegar, soy sauce, sugar and coffee crystals. Bring to a boil over medium-high heat. Boil for 2-5 minutes, or until reduced to 2 tablespoons.

Arrange the asparagus on a serving platter. Drizzle the sauce evenly over the top. Serve immediately. Makes 4 servings.

Grilled Corn with Smokehouse Maple Chipotle Butter
McCormick

½ cup (1 stick) butter, softened

2 tablespoons McCormick Grill Mates Smokehouse Maple Seasoning

2 tablespoons maple syrup

½ teaspoon McCormick Gourmet Collection chipotle chile pepper

8 ears fresh corn

Preheat the grill.

In a small bowl, mix butter, maple seasoning, maple syrup and chipotle chile pepper until well blended. Set aside.

Remove husks and silk strands from the corn.

Grill the corn over medium-high heat for 10 minutes, or until tender and lightly charred, turning occasionally.

Spread the butter mixture over the corn. Serve immediately. Makes 8 servings.

Nutritional information: Each serving has 220 calories, 3 g protein, 25 g carbohydrates, 12 g fat, 30 mg cholesterol, 2 g fiber, 417 mg sodium.

Roasted Asparagus with Pistachios

Grower Direct Marketing/Victoria Island Farms

2 pounds asparagus, trimmed
2 tablespoons olive oil
Salt and pepper

½ cup pistachios, shelled and chopped
½ cup grated Parmesan cheese

Preheat oven to 425°F.

Place asparagus on a baking sheet and drizzle with oil. Toss to coat. Season to taste with salt and pepper. Arrange the asparagus in a single layer on the baking sheet.

Roast on the center oven rack for 10 minutes. Remove the asparagus from the oven and sprinkle with pistachios and Parmesan. Return to the oven for 5 minutes. Serve immediately. Makes 6 servings.

Sautéed Baby Bok Choy and Broccoli Florets

Babé Farms/Gold Coast Packing

1 pound Babé Farms
   baby bok choy
1 pound Gold Coast
   broccoli florets
2 tablespoons vegetable oil
1 garlic clove, chopped
1 tablespoon finely grated
   fresh ginger
1-2 tablespoons soy sauce
Toasted sesame seeds,
   for garnish

Slice baby bok choy into 1-inch pieces. Coarsely chop the green leaves.

In a large skillet, boil ½ cup water. Add the chopped baby bok choy leaves and broccoli florets. Cover and simmer over medium-low heat until the broccoli is bright green, 5-7 minutes. Uncover and cook over high heat until the water evaporates, 2-4 minutes.

Add the baby bok choy pieces, oil and garlic. Cook, tossing often, until the garlic is fragrant, about 2 minutes.

Press ginger in a sieve over the skillet to release the juices. Stir in soy sauce.

Sprinkle with toasted sesame seeds and serve. Makes 4-6 servings.

Fresh Tomato Lemon Pasta with Walnuts, Olives and Feta

Better Than Bouillon

2 teaspoons salt
1 cup Kirkland Signature
   Chardonnay
1 tablespoon butter
1 tablespoon olive oil
1 tablespoon Better Than
   Bouillon All-Natural
   Reduced Sodium
   Chicken Base
1 tablespoon
   all-purpose flour
½ cup half-and-half
2 teaspoons freshly
   grated lemon zest
½ teaspoon white pepper
1 pound penne pasta
1 cup walnuts,
   coarsely chopped
8 ounces grape
   tomatoes, halved
4 ounces feta cheese,
   crumbled
2 tablespoons chopped
   fresh basil
½ cup pitted, sliced
   Kalamata olives

In a large pot, combine 4 quarts of water and salt; bring to a boil for pasta.

In a small saucepan, simmer wine over medium heat until reduced by half.

In a medium saucepan, combine butter, oil, chicken base and flour. Cook and whisk over low heat for 1 minute. Slowly whisk in half-and-half and cook until the sauce thickens. Whisk in reduced wine, lemon zest and pepper.

Cook pasta until al dente. Reserve ½ cup pasta water, then drain the pasta. Place in a serving bowl.

Reheat the sauce and whisk in reserved pasta water. Pour over the pasta and toss. Add walnuts, tomatoes, feta and basil; gently toss. Garnish with olives. Makes 8 servings.

Lemony Quinoa with Maple-Glazed Pistachios

Kirkland Signature/Setton Pistachio/Setton Farms

2 cups water

½ teaspoon sea salt, divided

½ cup brown quinoa

½ cup red quinoa

10-12 fresh basil leaves, finely chopped

2 carrots, finely grated

½ teaspoon finely ground black pepper

¼ teaspoon ground chipotle pepper

1 teaspoon maple syrup or agave nectar

1 tablespoon Dijon mustard

Grated zest of 1 lemon

2 tablespoons fresh lemon juice

1 tablespoon extra-virgin olive oil

MAPLE-GLAZED PISTACHIOS

2 teaspoons neutral-tasting oil

1 tablespoon maple syrup

½ cup Kirkland Signature roasted, salted California pistachio nuts, shelled

¼ teaspoon sea salt

¼ teaspoon finely ground black pepper

Cayenne pepper to taste (optional)

Place water in a medium pot and bring to a boil. Add ¼ teaspoon salt. Meanwhile, dry-roast quinoa in a sauté pan over medium heat, stirring until fragrant, about 3-4 minutes. Add quinoa to the boiling water, lower the heat to medium-low and cook, partially covered, for 14-15 minutes, or until all the liquid is absorbed.

Prepare the pistachios: Place oil and maple syrup in a small sauté pan over medium heat. Stir and cook about 30 seconds. Add pistachios, salt, pepper and cayenne. Cook until the pistachios are well glazed, about 2-3 minutes. Remove from the heat and let cool slightly.

In a large bowl, combine basil, carrots, cooked quinoa, ¼ teaspoon salt, pepper, chipotle, maple syrup, mustard, lemon zest and juice, oil and the pistachios.

Serve warm or at room temperature. Makes 4 servings.

Recipe courtesy of Jenny Engel and Heather Goldberg – sisters, authors, co-owners of Spork Foods, www.sporkfoods.com.

Bow-Tie Pasta with Fresh Tomatoes

Mastronardi Produce/SUNSET

2 pounds SUNSET Campari cocktail tomatoes
½ cup chopped fresh basil
¼ cup extra-virgin olive oil
2-3 garlic cloves, minced

1 teaspoon salt
¼-½ teaspoon crushed red pepper flakes
½ teaspoon freshly ground black pepper
1 pound dry bow-tie pasta
1 cup freshly grated Parmesan cheese

Cut tomatoes in half and lightly squeeze the juice into a bowl. Chop the tomatoes and add to the bowl. Add basil, oil, garlic, salt, red pepper flakes and black pepper.

Mix, cover and let sit at room temperature for 15 minutes for the flavors to marry.

Meanwhile, cook pasta according to package directions. Drain well.

Toss the hot pasta with the tomato sauce and Parmesan. Adjust the seasoning to taste. Serve immediately. Makes 6 servings.

Lemony Herbed Orzo
Paramount Citrus

- **2 cups dry orzo pasta**
- **2 tablespoons butter**
- **1 tablespoon extra-virgin olive oil**
- **1 tablespoon finely minced shallots**
- **½ cup chopped fresh Italian parsley**
- **¼ cup thinly sliced chives**
- **1 tablespoon chopped fresh basil or tarragon**
- **3 tablespoons fresh-squeezed Paramount Citrus lemon juice**
- **1 tablespoon finely minced lemon zest (see note)**
- **¾ teaspoon kosher salt**
- **Freshly ground black pepper**
- **⅓ cup grated Parmesan cheese**

Bring 3 quarts of water to a boil in a large pot. Stir in orzo and cook for about 6-8 minutes, stirring often, until just al dente. Immediately drain well.

Return the orzo to the pot and stir in butter, oil, shallots and herbs. Then stir in lemon juice, zest, seasonings and cheese. Makes 6-8 servings.

Note: Zest is the outer peel of the fruit—with no white pith attached. You can remove the zest from the fruit with a fine zesting tool that makes long, pretty strands, or you can peel off the zest with an ordinary potato peeler, being careful not to get any white pith, and then finely mince it.

Recipe developed by Kathy Casey Food Studios for Paramount Citrus.

Easy Herb and Cheese Potato Soufflé
Alsum Farms & Produce, Inc./RPE

- **1½ pounds Wisconsin russet potatoes, peeled and quartered**
- **2 tablespoons unsalted butter**
- **¾ cup half-and-half**
- **¾ cup grated Parmesan cheese**
- **1¼ cups grated Swiss cheese**
- **1 tablespoon chopped fresh parsley**
- **1 teaspoon chopped fresh oregano**
- **1 teaspoon chopped fresh thyme**
- **Salt and pepper**
- **5 large egg yolks**
- **7 large egg whites**
- **⅛ teaspoon cream of tartar**

Preheat oven to 375°F. Grease and flour a 2-quart ceramic baking dish.

Simmer potatoes for 20 minutes, or until tender. Drain, then return to the pan to dry for 1 minute. Remove from the heat.

Add butter and mash the potatoes. Stir in half-and-half. Let cool slightly. Stir in cheese, herbs, and salt and pepper to taste. Stir in yolks. Transfer to a large bowl.

In another large bowl, beat whites with a mixer until foamy. Add cream of tartar and beat until stiff peaks form. Stir ⅓ of the whites into the potatoes. Fold in remaining whites until no streaks remain. Pour into the baking dish.

Bake in bottom third of oven for 45 minutes, or until puffed and golden. Don't open the oven during cooking time. Makes 6-8 servings.

Garlic Buttermilk Mashed Potatoes
Skagit Valley's Best Produce/Valley Pride/Wallace Farms

2 pounds Washington red potatoes
1 tablespoon kosher salt
1 tablespoon chopped garlic
½ cup unsalted butter
½ cup low-fat buttermilk

Wash potatoes and scrub clean if needed (do not peel). Cut into roughly 1-inch pieces.

Place in a pot and cover with water. Add salt and bring to a rolling boil. Boil, uncovered, for about 15 minutes, or until soft. Drain the potatoes in a strainer, then return them to the pot and keep covered.

In a saucepan, combine garlic, butter and buttermilk; bring to a simmer.

Mash the potatoes with a potato masher until smooth. Add the hot buttermilk to the potatoes and mix to blend.

Cover with parchment paper and keep warm on a double boiler until ready to serve. Makes 6 servings.

Recipe developed by Kaspars Special Events & Catering.

Parmesan Roasted Steakhouse Potatoes
MountainKing Potatoes

2 pounds MountainKing Steakhouse Roaster potatoes
3 tablespoons olive oil
1½ teaspoons kosher salt
¼ teaspoon black pepper
1 cup grated Parmesan cheese
2 tablespoons chopped fresh rosemary

Preheat oven to 400°F.

Wash potatoes, then cut into quarters lengthwise.

In a large bowl, combine remaining ingredients. Add the potatoes and toss well to coat.

Spread in an even layer on a baking sheet and place in the oven. Roast for approximately 45 minutes, turning once, until the potatoes are golden brown and crisp. Makes 4-6 servings.

Grilled Southwestern Potatoes

Farm Fresh Direct/Top Brass Marketing

3-4 pounds fingerling potatoes
  or B-size red potatoes
¼ cup olive oil
3 tablespoons ground cumin
2 tablespoons chili powder
2 tablespoons garlic powder
1 teaspoon cayenne pepper (optional)
Cooking spray
Salt (optional)

Preheat the grill.

Cut potatoes into bite-size chunks and cook in the microwave for about 10 minutes, or until tender. Place the potatoes in a large bowl. Add oil and stir to coat. Mix the spices together. Add to the potatoes and blend well.

Place the potatoes in a grilling basket coated with cooking spray. Use a shallow baking sheet if you don't have a grilling basket.

Place on the grill and cook at 250-300°F for about 30 minutes, stirring frequently, until most of the potatoes are browned and crispy. Add salt if desired. Makes 6-8 servings.

Tangerine Coleslaw
Florida Classic Growers/Noble Worldwide Citrus

1 small head of cabbage, cut in long thin shreds

3 Florida tangerines, segmented

½ cup raisins

¼ cup chopped nuts (walnuts work best)

DRESSING

¼ cup salad oil

Grated zest of ½ Florida tangerine

¼ cup fresh Florida tangerine juice

Juice of ½ fresh lemon

2 tablespoons honey

1 tablespoon toasted sesame seeds

Prepare the dressing: In a jar with a lid, combine oil, tangerine zest and juice, lemon juice, honey and sesame seeds; shake well.

In a large bowl, combine cabbage, tangerine segments, raisins and the dressing; toss to blend. Chill.

To serve, add chopped nuts and toss gently. Makes 6 servings.

Variation: Substitute oranges for the tangerines.

Grilled Peaches
I.M. Ripe

2 tablespoons extra-fine sugar

2 tablespoons brandy

4 I.M. Ripe peaches, cut in half, stone removed

2 tablespoons olive oil

Sprinkle sugar and brandy on a cookie sheet.

Place peaches face down on the sugar mixture and let macerate for 30-60 minutes.

Preheat the grill to high.

When ready to cook, coat the exposed fruit flesh lightly with oil. Grill over high heat until grill marks appear and the flesh softens. Makes 4 servings.

Tip: Serve alongside a salad, chicken or grilled steak.

Ham-Stuffed Apples
Borton & Sons

6 large Borton & Sons red apples, unpeeled
8 ounces cooked ham, cut into small cubes
2 tablespoons butter, softened
⅓ cup raisins (brown or golden)

⅓ cup pecans, chopped
3 tablespoons light brown sugar
½-1 cup apple juice

Preheat oven to 350°F.

Cut the tops off the apples and scoop out the core plus some of the fruit, but be sure to leave a thick shell to hold the stuffing.

Chop the fruit that was removed from the apples, to yield approximately 1 cup.

In a mixing bowl, combine the chopped apple with ham, butter, raisins, pecans and brown sugar, stirring to combine well. Spoon the mixture into the cored apples and place them in a baking dish.

Pour juice over the apples and bake for 35-40 minutes, or until the apples are tender, basting occasionally with the juice. Makes 6 servings.

Salads

Chicken and Orange Rice Salad
Sunkist Growers

2 cups water

1 chicken bouillon cube

Grated zest of
½ Sunkist lemon

1 cup uncooked regular
white rice

1½ cups cubed
cooked chicken

1 2.25-ounce can sliced ripe
(black) olives, drained

¼ cup sliced green onions

2 Sunkist oranges,
peeled and cut into
half-cartwheel slices

Salad greens, for serving

FRESH ORANGE DRESSING

2 Sunkist oranges, juiced

½ cup vegetable oil

1 teaspoon celery salt

1 teaspoon dried tarragon
leaves, crushed

¼ teaspoon paprika

In a saucepan, bring water to a boil with the bouillon cube and lemon zest. Add rice and return to a boil. Reduce the heat, cover and simmer for 20 minutes, or until the liquid has been absorbed. Let cool slightly.

Prepare the dressing: In a jar with a lid, combine all the ingredients and shake well.

In a bowl, combine the rice, chicken, olives, green onions and orange slices. Toss gently with the dressing; cover and chill.

To serve, arrange on salad greens on individual serving plates. Makes 4 servings.

Sunkist

Chicken Salad with Fruit and Nuts

Kirkland Signature

4 cups cooked chicken
cut in 1-inch cubes

1½ cups Kirkland Signature
Wholesome Fruit & Nuts

½ cup mayonnaise

½ cup sour cream

¼ cup bottled chutney

1 tablespoon lemon juice

½ teaspoon salt

⅛ teaspoon ground pepper

Salad greens, torn into
bite-size pieces

In a large bowl, combine chicken and fruit and nut mix.

In another bowl, combine mayonnaise, sour cream, chutney, lemon juice, salt and pepper. Add to the chicken mixture and toss well. Cover and chill to allow the flavors to blend.

Serve on a bed of salad greens. Makes 6 servings.

Nectarine and Ahi Tuna Salad
I.M. Ripe

3 I.M. Ripe nectarines:
   2 pitted and cut into
   cubes, 1 pitted and
   thinly sliced

1 pound fresh ahi tuna,
   cut into cubes

1 avocado, pitted,
   peeled and diced

2 green onions, thinly sliced

1 handful of fresh cilantro,
   finely chopped

1 tablespoon black
   sesame seeds

Coarse-grind salt

4 cups mixed spring greens

2 tablespoons seasoned
   rice vinegar

1 tablespoon sesame
   seed oil

DRESSING

2 tablespoons fresh
   lime juice

1 tablespoon seasoned
   rice vinegar

1 tablespoon coconut milk

1 teaspoon grated
   fresh ginger

1 teaspoon grated
   lime zest

1 teaspoon minced fresh
   serrano chile

½ teaspoon
   prepared wasabi

½ teaspoon salt

1 tablespoon sesame
   seed oil

Prepare the dressing: In a medium bowl, combine lime juice, vinegar, coconut milk, ginger, lime zest, chile, wasabi and salt. Whisk in oil until blended. Set aside.

In a large bowl, combine the cubed nectarines, ahi, avocado, green onions, cilantro and sesame seeds. Add the dressing and gently mix. Season to taste with salt.

Place spring greens in a medium bowl. Whisk together vinegar and oil in a small bowl. Drizzle onto the greens. Toss to coat.

Divide the greens among 4 plates. Garnish each plate with nectarine slices and top with the nectarine/ahi mixture. Makes 4 servings.

Recipe created by Peggy Thurlow.

Tuna Salad with Grapes
Four Star Fruit

2 5-ounce cans solid white
   tuna, well-drained

2 hard-boiled eggs,
   coarsely chopped

2 celery stalks, finely
   chopped (about ½ cup)

1 tablespoon chopped
   fresh tarragon

20 Four Star Fruit red
   seedless grapes,
   cut in half, divided

20 Four Star Fruit green
   seedless grapes,
   cut in half, divided

1 teaspoon grated
   lemon zest

2 tablespoons mayonnaise

2 tablespoons sour cream

3 tablespoons fresh
   lemon juice

½ teaspoon salt

4 cups shredded cabbage

In a bowl, combine tuna, eggs, celery, tarragon and ¾ of the grapes. Toss with a fork.

In another bowl, whisk lemon zest, mayonnaise, sour cream, lemon juice and salt. Add to the tuna salad and toss to coat.

To serve, place 1 cup of shredded cabbage on each plate. Top with tuna salad. Garnish with the remaining grapes. Makes 4 servings.

Tuna and Apple Salad in Apple Cups

Stemilt Growers

1 6-ounce can white albacore tuna
    (packed in water), drained

1 tablespoon honey mustard

2-3 tablespoons mayonnaise
    (or Vegenaise)

⅓ cup diced celery

2 tablespoons diced red onion

2 Stemilt apples, of your choice

1 lemon

Kosher salt and ground black
    pepper, to taste

Place drained tuna in a bowl. Stir in mustard, mayonnaise, celery and onion. Set aside.

Slice off the top quarter of each apple. Cut an additional slice from each apple bottom (¼-½ inch thick). Rub the cut sides of each apple, as well as the cut slices, with fresh-cut lemon to help prevent browning; set aside on a paper towel to dry.

Use a spoon to carefully carve out the inside of the apples. Beginning in the center, remove and discard the core. Then continue scooping out flesh, working toward the perimeter, leaving about a ⅜- to ½-inch edge. Place the apples on the paper towel and drizzle the flesh with lemon juice.

Transfer the apple trimmings to a cutting board and dice into ¼-inch pieces, working around any remaining core. Add to the tuna mixture and combine well. Add a scant sprinkle of salt and pepper to taste; mix well.

Place the apples on a plate, fill each with about ½ cup of the salad mixture and cap with the stemmed apple tops. Serve immediately. Makes 2 servings.

Recipe developed by Lorie Hopcus for Stemilt Growers.

Stemilt
World Famous Fruit

Lobster Salad with Tamarind Vinaigrette

Pescanova

3 Pescanova frozen lobster tails

3½ ounces baby lettuce

4 ounces avocado balls

2 ounces fresh hearts of palm, sliced

1½ ounces Roma tomatoes, sliced

⅔ cup chopped fresh cilantro

Salt and pepper

1 tablespoon freshly shaved
  coconut, toasted

TAMARIND VINAIGRETTE

½ cup olive oil

½ cup white balsamic vinegar

1 tablespoon Dijon mustard

8 ounces tamarind paste

1 pinch salt

1 pinch brown sugar

Prepare the lobster: Thaw lobsters in cold running water. Add 3 tablespoons salt to a large pot of water and bring to a boil. Drop lobsters into the boiling water.

When the water returns to a boil, cook for 3 minutes. Transfer the lobsters to a bowl filled with iced water for 3 minutes. Remove meat from shells using scissors. Chop meat into large chunks. Set aside.

Prepare the vinaigrette: Mix all ingredients until well blended. Set aside.

Place lettuce in a serving bowl. In a mixing bowl, combine lobster, avocado, hearts of palm, tomatoes and cilantro. Season lightly with salt and pepper. Add vinaigrette to taste and toss.

Arrange the lobster mixture on top of the lettuce and garnish with coconut. Makes 4 servings.

Fire and Ice Pasta Salad
MorningStar Farms

4 ounces dried penne pasta

2 MorningStar Farms Chipotle Black Bean Burgers

2 medium mangoes, peeled, seeded and coarsely chopped

1 medium tomato, seeded and coarsely chopped

1 medium jalapeño, seeded and finely chopped

⅓ cup picante sauce

2 tablespoons lime juice

1 tablespoon honey

1 teaspoon olive oil

Lettuce leaves, for serving

Cook pasta according to package directions. Drain. Rinse with cold water and drain again.

Cook burgers according to package directions. Cut each patty into bite-size pieces.

In a large bowl, gently toss together the pasta, burgers, mangoes, tomato and jalapeño. Cover and refrigerate for 2 hours.

Meanwhile, in a small bowl whisk together picante sauce, lime juice, honey and oil. Drizzle over the chilled salad. Lightly toss to coat.

To serve, line 4 plates with lettuce leaves. Top with salad. Makes 4 servings.

Autumn Apple Salad with Creamy Maple Dressing
Borton & Sons

5 ounces mixed baby greens

2 Borton & Sons Gala or Red Delicious apples, cored and cut into bite-size pieces

½ cup dried cranberries

½ cup chopped walnuts, toasted (see note)

DRESSING

½ cup canola oil

¼ cup maple syrup

¼ cup mayonnaise

2 tablespoons white wine vinegar

2 teaspoons sugar

Salt and pepper to taste

In a salad bowl, combine baby greens, apples, cranberries and walnuts.

Prepare the dressing: Combine all ingredients and whisk until well blended.

Add the dressing to the salad and toss to blend. Makes 4 servings.

Note: To toast walnuts, place in a dry nonstick skillet over medium heat for 3-5 minutes, stirring occasionally. Cool before adding to the salad.

Crunchy Harvest Salad with Honey Cider Vinaigrette
Paramount Farms

2 heads Belgian endive

6 cups mixed greens

1 apple, thinly sliced

3 ounces goat cheese

¾ cup Wonderful Almond Accents Sweet Roasted Almonds with Pomegranate*

HONEY CIDER VINAIGRETTE

2 tablespoons apple cider vinegar

1 tablespoon honey

2 teaspoons Dijon mustard

¼ cup olive oil

¼ teaspoon kosher salt

Freshly ground black pepper

*If not available, use Wonderful Almond Accents Honey Roasted with Cranberries.

Prepare the vinaigrette: In a large bowl, whisk together all ingredients.

Core endives and slice lengthwise into thin strips.

Add the endive, greens and apple to the bowl and toss with the vinaigrette to coat well.

Serve the salad on a large platter or on individual plates. Top with crumbled goat cheese and Wonderful Almond Accents. Makes 4 servings.

Tip: For the holidays, try adding a pinch of ground nutmeg or cinnamon to the vinaigrette.

Recipe developed by Kathy Casey Food Studios for Wonderful Almond Accents.

Pear Bistro Salad

California Pear Advisory Board

8 cups assorted mixed salad greens

2 fresh California Bartlett or Comice pears, cored and sliced

½ red onion, thinly sliced

½ cup walnut halves

½ cup crumbled blue cheese

Balsamic vinegar

Olive oil

Line a large platter with salad greens. Top with pears and sliced onion. Sprinkle with walnuts and crumbled cheese.

Combine vinegar and oil to taste. Drizzle over the salad.

Serve with crusty bread, if desired. Makes 4 servings.

CALIFORNIA
PEARS

Green and Red Grape Spinach Salad

Four Star Fruit

¼ cup red wine vinegar

1 garlic clove, minced

1 tablespoon Dijon mustard

1 tablespoon sugar

Salt and pepper

½ cup olive oil

4 cups fresh spinach

2 cups fresh arugula

½ cup crumbled Roquefort cheese

4 slices bacon, cooked, drained and crumbled

¼ cup toasted chopped pecans

30 Four Star Fruit green seedless grapes

30 Four Star Fruit red seedless grapes

In a small bowl, whisk together vinegar, garlic, mustard, sugar, and salt and pepper to taste. Add oil in a steady stream, whisking until the dressing is emulsified.

In a large bowl, combine spinach, arugula, Roquefort, bacon, pecans and grapes. Toss the salad with the dressing. Makes 4 servings.

Double Blue Spinach Salad
Taylor Fresh

3 slices thick-cut bacon

½ cup diced yellow onion

¾ cup sliced mushrooms (shiitake if available)

6 cups Taylor Fresh organic baby spinach

¼ cup crumbled blue cheese

¼ cup sliced almonds

1 cup blueberries, rinsed

DRESSING

¼ cup extra-virgin olive oil

3 tablespoons balsamic vinegar

½ teaspoon apple cider vinegar

¼ teaspoon crushed garlic

Salt and cracked pepper

In a frying pan, cook bacon over medium heat until golden brown. Remove bacon from the pan. Pour out excess bacon grease—do not clean or wipe out the pan. Add onion and sauté over medium heat until golden brown, about 3-4 minutes.

Prepare the dressing: In a mixing bowl, combine oil, vinegars and garlic. Whisk to blend. Season to taste with salt and pepper. Add the sautéed onion to the dressing and gently stir.

In the same frying pan, sauté mushrooms for 2-3 minutes over medium heat.

Place spinach in a large salad bowl. Drizzle with dressing and mix. Crumble bacon over the salad and add cheese, sautéed mushrooms, almonds and blueberries. Mix thoroughly.

Serve immediately. Makes 6 servings.

Feta and Strawberry Salad
Président

2 tablespoons white wine vinegar

2 tablespoons balsamic vinegar

¼ cup sugar

¼ teaspoon mustard powder

Salt

1 garlic clove, peeled and minced

1 head of Bibb lettuce

6 fresh strawberries, sliced

¼ cup walnuts

4 ounces Président feta cheese, crumbled

To prepare the dressing, combine vinegars and sugar in a saucepan. Cook over medium heat, stirring, until the sugar dissolves. Do not boil. Remove from the heat and add mustard powder and a pinch of salt. Whisk vigorously until well blended. Add garlic, then stir briefly. Let cool.

Arrange lettuce leaves on plates. Add strawberries and walnuts. Sprinkle with feta. Drizzle with dressing to taste. Makes 2 servings.

Grilled Artisan Romaine and Onion Salad
Tanimura & Antle

2 heads Tanimura & Antle Artisan Romaine or Romaine Hearts

¾ cup balsamic vinegar

2 Artisan Sweet Italian Red Onions, sliced into ¼-inch rings

2 tablespoons extra-virgin olive oil, divided

Sea salt and freshly ground pepper

2 tablespoons shaved Romano cheese

Preheat an outdoor grill or a stovetop grill pan to high.

Wash lettuce and cut heads in half lengthwise; drain cut-side down.

Place vinegar in a saucepan and cook over medium heat until reduced to ¼ cup. Cover to keep warm and set aside.

Brush onion rings with some of the oil and season to taste with salt and pepper. Place on the hot grill and cook on 1 side for 3 minutes. Turn and grill for another 2 minutes. Set aside.

Brush cut side of the romaine with oil; season to taste with salt and pepper. Place cut-side down on the grill and cook for 3 minutes, or until light char marks appear.

To serve, sprinkle the romaine with shaved cheese. Top with onion rings and drizzle with balsamic glaze. Makes 4 servings.

Caesar Salad
Foxy Vegetables

2 medium Foxy romaine hearts or organic Foxy romaine hearts

1 large egg yolk

1 teaspoon Worcestershire sauce

2 tablespoons fresh lemon juice

1 medium garlic clove, crushed

Pinch of salt

½ teaspoon freshly ground pepper

1½ teaspoons anchovy paste or 4 flat anchovies, minced

1 teaspoon Dijon mustard

2 teaspoons balsamic vinegar

⅓ cup extra-virgin olive oil

⅔ cup freshly grated Parmesan cheese, divided, plus more for garnish

Croutons (optional)

Rinse romaine. Tear into 2- to 3-inch pieces. Place in a large bowl. Set aside.

In a blender, combine egg yolk, Worcestershire sauce, lemon juice, garlic, salt, pepper, anchovy, mustard and vinegar. Process for 30-45 seconds, or until the mixture is smooth. With the blender running, slowly pour in oil, continuing to blend until emulsified. Stir in ⅓ cup Parmesan.

Add half of the dressing to the romaine hearts and toss well. Add the remaining ⅓ cup Parmesan to the remaining dressing, add to the salad, and toss again. Add croutons if desired.

Serve immediately, with extra Parmesan for garnish. Makes 4-6 servings.

Kale Salad with Meyer Lemon Vinaigrette
Duda Farm Fresh Foods

3 tablespoons Meyer lemon juice, squeezed from 1 Meyer lemon

½ teaspoon ground cumin

½ teaspoon sea salt

3-4 grinds of black pepper

2 teaspoons extra-virgin olive oil

4 lightly packed cups curly kale cut into bite-size pieces

½ cup sweet onion cut into thin crescents

¼ cup pomegranate seeds or dried cranberries

2 tablespoons raw pumpkin seeds

In a large bowl, combine the first 4 ingredients. When the salt dissolves, mix in oil. Add kale and toss for 1 minute to coat well.

Scatter onion, then pomegranate seeds (or dried cranberries), over the kale.

Heat a heavy skillet over medium-high heat. Add pumpkin seeds to the dry pan. Cook, shaking the pan frequently, until the seeds start to color and swell, about 1 minute. Scatter the toasted pumpkin seeds over the salad.

Toss the salad and serve. Makes 4 servings.

Rainbow Rabe Salad
Andy Boy

1 bunch Andy Boy broccoli rabe

¼ cup sliced yellow bell pepper

¼ cup sliced red bell pepper

¼ cup thinly sliced red onion (or to taste)

½ cup cherry tomatoes, cut in half

Handful of crumbled Point Reyes blue cheese

VINAIGRETTE

¼ cup red wine vinegar

¼ cup water

¼ teaspoon sugar

Juice of ⅛ lemon

½ teaspoon salt

¼ teaspoon ground black pepper

¼ teaspoon Worcestershire sauce

¼ teaspoon Colman's English mustard

½ garlic clove, minced

1 cup light extra-virgin olive oil

Blanch broccoli rabe for 5 minutes in boiling water. Plunge into ice water and let cool. Drain and let dry.

Prepare the vinaigrette: In a mixer with a whisk attachment, combine all ingredients except the olive oil. Blend well for 30 seconds. With the mixer on medium speed, slowly drizzle in the oil until well combined. Refrigerate in an airtight container until ready to use.

In a salad bowl, combine broccoli rabe, bell peppers, onion, tomatoes and cheese. Add vinaigrette to taste and toss to blend. Makes 2-4 servings.

Caprese Pasta Salad with Avocado

Chilean Hass Avocados

1 pound penne pasta

⅓ cup extra-virgin olive oil, divided

3 large Chilean Hass avocados, halved, pitted, peeled and cut into ½-inch cubes

Juice of ½ lemon

16 fresh mozzarella bocconcini (bite-size), halved

12 cherry tomatoes, halved

1 bunch fresh basil, thinly sliced (reserve several sprigs for garnish)

Salt and pepper

Cook pasta in a large pot of boiling salted water until tender but still firm, stirring occasionally. Drain well. In a large bowl, toss pasta with half of the olive oil.

Meanwhile, in a small bowl gently toss avocado cubes with lemon juice.

Add the avocado cubes to the pasta, along with the mozzarella, tomatoes, sliced basil and remaining olive oil. Mix gently to blend. Season to taste with salt and pepper.

Garnish with basil sprigs and serve. Makes 4-6 servings.

Tomato, Basil and Buffalo Mozzarella Salad

Houweling's Tomatoes

6 Houweling's Roma tomatoes (see note)

5-6 ounces (150 grams) buffalo mozzarella (or bocconcini)

6 basil leaves

3 tablespoons extra-virgin olive oil

Salt

Freshly ground pepper

Cut tomatoes into wedges.

Rip mozzarella into bite-size pieces.

Tear basil leaves into pieces.

Arrange the tomatoes and mozzarella on a plate. Sprinkle with basil. Drizzle with olive oil and season to taste with salt and pepper. Makes 3-4 servings.

Note: Remember, tomatoes taste best at room temperature, so don't put them in the refrigerator!

Grilled Eggplant and Tomato Salad
Windset Farms

4 ounces aged Manchego cheese,
  finely grated

2 tablespoons finely sliced
  Italian parsley

Grated zest of 1 lemon

Cracked black pepper

2 cups canola oil

10 garlic cloves

½ cup sherry vinegar

1 tablespoon Keen's mustard powder

3 Adagio baby eggplants

Kosher salt

4 Virtuoso beefsteak tomatoes

4 leaves Delicato butter lettuce
  or romaine hearts, for serving

Crusty bread, for serving

Combine cheese with parsley, lemon zest and pepper to taste. Set aside and keep at room temperature.

In a small saucepan, start simmering canola oil with garlic cloves over medium heat. After 12-15 minutes, remove from the heat and let cool; the garlic should be golden brown and translucent. Strain and keep the oil. Place the garlic cloves in a small dish; refrigerate if not using right away.

Place garlic oil in a bowl, saving 2 tablespoons for brushing the eggplant. Add vinegar and mustard powder to the bowl and whisk to combine. Set aside. Preheat and clean the grill, barbecue or griddle.

Slice eggplant into disks approximately ½ inch thick. Brush with garlic oil and season to taste with salt and pepper. Grill over medium-high heat until tender (about 3 minutes per side). Remove and let cool.

Slice tomatoes into disks. Layer with the eggplant. Pour on dressing to taste, add garlic cloves and garnish with the cheese/parsley mixture. Serve with lettuce and some crusty bread. Makes 2-4 servings.

Note: Extra dressing will keep, refrigerated, for a month.

Recipe developed by chef Ned Bell.

Wild Rice Salad with Apples and Walnuts
Domex Superfresh Growers

1 cup wild rice

¼ cup olive oil

2 tablespoons red wine vinegar

1 teaspoon Dijon mustard

Salt and freshly ground black pepper

1 Superfresh Growers Gala apple, cored and finely diced

½ cup thinly sliced celery (preferably from tender center stalks)

½ cup chopped toasted walnuts

In a medium saucepan, bring 3 cups of salted water to a boil. Stir in rice, reduce the heat to low, cover and simmer until the rice is tender and puffed, 30-35 minutes. Drain well and set aside to cool slightly.

In a large bowl, combine oil, vinegar and mustard with a good pinch each of salt and pepper. Stir with a fork until well blended. Add the warm (not hot) wild rice and gently toss to evenly coat with the dressing. Let sit for 30 minutes to fully cool and allow the flavors to meld.

Add apple, celery and walnuts; toss to mix. Taste the salad for seasoning, adding more salt or pepper if needed.

Serve right away, or cover and refrigerate for up to 4 hours. Let the salad come to room temperature before serving. The walnuts will be at their crispest if held aside and stirred into the salad just before serving. Makes 4-6 servings.

Dried Plum Rice Salad
Kirkland Signature/Sunsweet

3 cups cooked long-grain brown or white rice, chilled

2 cups lightly packed chopped fresh spinach

½ cup Kirkland Signature/ Sunsweet dried plums, chopped

½ cup diced bell pepper (preferably red)

½ cup slivered almonds, toasted

⅓ cup sliced green onions

6 strips crisp cooked bacon, crumbled

DRESSING

⅓ cup extra-virgin olive oil

⅓ cup rice vinegar (not seasoned)

1 tablespoon sugar

1 tablespoon soy sauce

2 garlic cloves, minced

Freshly ground pepper to taste

In a large bowl, stir together rice, spinach, dried plums, bell pepper, almonds, green onions and bacon.

Prepare the dressing: In a small bowl, whisk together all the ingredients.

Drizzle the dressing over the salad. Toss well to coat. Refrigerate for at least 1 hour. Makes 8 servings.

Tip: This can be prepared 1 day ahead. Add the spinach and almonds just before serving.

Avocado Summer Fruit Salad with Honey-Lemon Dressing
AJ Trucco/Blossom Hill/Fillmore-Piru Citrus/ Nature's Partner/Mulholland Citrus/ The Oppenheimer Group

½ cup fresh lemon juice

2 tablespoons olive oil

1 teaspoon poppy seeds

⅓ cup honey

Salt to taste (optional)

1 mango, peeled, pitted and cubed

1 cup seedless grapes, halved

1 cup fresh blueberries

2 easy-peel clementine or Murcott oranges, peeled and sectioned

2 kiwifruit, peeled and diced

1 avocado, peeled, pitted and cubed

In a mixing bowl, combine lemon juice, oil, poppy seeds, honey and salt. Beat with a rotary beater until smooth.

Arrange fruits on a plate and drizzle with the dressing.

Chill until ready to serve. Makes 4 servings.

Waldorf Celebration Salad

Columbia Marketing International

½ cup sour cream
½ cup mayonnaise
½ cup orange juice concentrate
3 CMI Ambrosia apples, cored and diced

3 CMI Granny Smith apples, cored and diced
½ cup chopped walnuts
1 cup chopped celery
2 pounds red and green seedless grapes
1 cup shredded coconut

In a small bowl, combine sour cream, mayonnaise and orange juice concentrate.

In a large bowl, toss together apples, walnuts, celery, grapes and coconut. Add the dressing and stir to coat. Cover and chill for at least an hour before serving. Makes 6 servings.

Recipe courtesy of chef David Toal of Ravenous Catering, Wenatchee, Washington.

Mojito Fruit Salad

Bee Sweet Citrus/Corona-College Heights/Datepac, LLC/Mas Melons & Grapes/Premier Citrus Marketing/Sun World

1 cup pink grapefruit pieces

1 cup Scarlotta Seedless red grapes

1 cup cubed cantaloupe

1 cup hulled and quartered strawberries

1 cup Medjool dates,
   halved and pits removed

1 cup fresh blueberries

3 sprigs fresh mint

2 teaspoons sugar

3 tablespoons fresh lime juice

Mix the fruit in a bowl with a tight-fitting lid. In a small bowl, stir together mint leaves, sugar and lime juice, crushing the mint with the back of a spoon while mixing to extract flavor. Pour over the fruit mixture. Seal the bowl with the lid and refrigerate for at least 1 hour.

Just before serving, gently flip the sealed bowl several times to coat the fruit with the dressing. Makes 6 servings.

Nutritional information: Each serving has 83 calories, 0.6 g fat, 0 mg cholesterol.

Chef's Choice

Top chefs are known for their ability to create delicious recipes that showcase not only fresh ingredients but also the cook's personality. We asked several of the best chefs around to work their magic with products from these great companies:

88

93

96

SEA·MAZZ

Karen Adler and Judith Fertig

Known as the BBQ Queens, Karen Adler and Judith Fertig are the authors of many barbecue cookbooks, including Fish & Shellfish, Grilled & Smoked *(Harvard Common Press, 2002) and their newest book,* The Gardener & the Grill *(Running Press, 2012). Visit them at* www.thebbqqueens.com.

Skewered Orange-Basted Shrimp on the Barbie recipe on page 86.

Skewered Orange-Basted Shrimp on the Barbie
SeaMazz

Recipes developed by Karen Adler and Judith Fertig

12 wooden skewers

2 pounds SeaMazz frozen jumbo (13- to 15-count) easy-peel shrimp, thawed

ORANGE-GINGER BASTE

¼ cup (4 tablespoons) unsalted butter, melted

1 cup freshly squeezed orange juice (from about 4 oranges)

1 teaspoon freshly grated orange zest

2 tablespoons freshly squeezed lime juice (from about 2 limes)

2 tablespoons dry sherry or rum (white or dark)

2 green onions, finely chopped with some of the green

2 teaspoons freshly grated ginger

Soak the skewers in water for 30 minutes.

Prepare the baste: In a bowl, whisk together melted butter, orange juice, orange zest, lime juice, sherry or rum, green onions and ginger. Reserve half to pass at the table.

Prepare a hot fire in your grill.

Thread shrimp onto the skewers. Brush liberally with the baste.

Grill the skewers for 2-4 minutes per side, basting again after turning, or until the shrimp is firm and opaque, with good grill marks. Serve the skewers drizzled with the reserved baste. Peel off the shells and eat.
Serves 6 as a main course, 12 as an appetizer.

Tip: Thread the shrimp onto the skewers without crowding, so they cook evenly.

Skewered Orange-Basted Shrimp on the Barbie photo on page 85.

Wood-Grilled Salmon with Honey Soy Glaze
SeaMazz

1 cup wood chips: alder, hickory, oak or mesquite

4 7-ounce SeaMazz frozen skinless salmon fillets, thawed

HONEY SOY GLAZE

2 tablespoons honey

2 tablespoons soy sauce

1 teaspoon lemon pepper

1 tablespoon vegetable oil

Prepare a medium-hot fire in your grill.

Prepare the glaze: In a bowl, whisk honey, soy sauce, lemon pepper and oil together.

Add a kiss of smoke. For a charcoal grill, throw 1 cup of water-soaked and drained wood chips on ashed-over coals. For a gas grill, place 1 cup dry wood chips on a piece of aluminum foil, create a packet and poke holes in the top of the packet before placing it near a heat source.

When you see the first wisp of smoke from the wood, place the salmon on the grill grates and close the lid of the grill. Grill for 3-4 minutes or until you can turn the fish easily and one side has good grill marks. Brush the grill-marked side with the glaze, close the lid and grill for 3-4 minutes more or until the fish is done to your liking. To serve, transfer the fish to a platter and drizzle with any remaining glaze. Makes 4 servings.

Venetian Grilled Lobster
SeaMazz

1 cup wood chips, preferably oak

4 9-ounce SeaMazz frozen raw lobster tails, thawed and kept refrigerated until used

Olive oil, for brushing and drizzling

Fresh lemon wedges

Chopped fresh Italian parsley, for garnish

Prepare a hot fire. For a charcoal grill, throw 1 cup of water-soaked and drained wood chips on ashed-over coals. For a gas grill, place 1 cup dry wood chips on a piece of aluminum foil, create a packet and poke holes in the top of the packet before placing near a heat source. Brush lobster tails on all sides with olive oil.

When you see the first wisp of smoke from the wood, place the tails on the grill, close the lid and grill for 6-8 minutes. Turn the lobster, close the lid again and grill again for 6-8 minutes, or until the lobster is opaque.

To remove the meat after the lobster is grilled, hold the lobster tail with a kitchen towel or your napkin in one hand and remove the meat using a fork in your other hand.

To serve, drizzle the lobster with olive oil and lemon juice and sprinkle with parsley. Makes 4 servings.

Tom Douglas

Tom Douglas creates deliciousness, served with graciousness at 13 different joints, all in Seattle. With more than 30 years dedicated to the Seattle restaurant scene, he is credited with putting the city on the culinary map. Douglas is the author of four cookbooks, including his latest title, The Dahlia Bakery Cookbook (Morrow, 2012). He was also recently named Outstanding Restaurateur 2012 by the James Beard Foundation.

ED ANDERSON

Pink Lady Apple and Radicchio Salad with Toasted Pecans

Rainier Fruit Company

Recipes developed by Tom Douglas

Try crumbling blue cheese over this crisp, colorful salad.

- 1½ teaspoons minced shallots
- 2 tablespoons sherry vinegar
- 1½ teaspoons honey
- 1½ teaspoons Dijon mustard
- 6 tablespoons olive oil
- Kosher salt and freshly ground black pepper
- 12 cups loosely packed arugula leaves, washed and dried
- ½ medium head radicchio, cored and leaves washed, dried and torn into bite-size pieces
- 1 Belgian endive, sliced in half, cored and cut into ½-inch strips
- 1½ Rainier Fruit Pink Lady apples, cored but not peeled
- ¼ lemon
- 1 cup pecan halves, toasted (see note)

To make the vinaigrette, combine shallots, vinegar, honey and mustard in a small bowl. Whisk in oil. Season to taste with salt and pepper.

In a large serving bowl, combine arugula, radicchio and endive. Cut apples into thin slices and add them to the bowl. Toss with enough vinaigrette to lightly coat everything, and season to taste with salt, pepper and a squeeze of lemon.

Sprinkle the pecans over the salad and serve. Makes 6 servings.

Note: Toast the pecans in a 375°F oven for 8-10 minutes, stirring occasionally, until fragrant and lightly browned.

Fresh Corn and Blueberry Relish

Rainier Fruit Company

Top grilled salmon fillets, chicken breasts or pork chops with generous spoonfuls of this light, refreshing relish.

- 2 teaspoons Champagne vinegar (or other mild vinegar)
- 1 teaspoon fresh lemon juice
- 2 teaspoons minced shallots
- 2 tablespoons extra-virgin olive oil
- Kosher salt and freshly ground black pepper
- 1 cup corn kernels, cut from the cob
- 5 cups loosely packed mâche or arugula leaves, washed and dried
- 1 cup fresh Rainier Fruit blueberries
- 3 tablespoons mint leaves torn into pieces
- 1 tablespoon thinly sliced chives

To make the vinaigrette, combine vinegar, lemon juice and shallots in a small bowl. Whisk in oil. Season to taste with salt and pepper.

Bring a small pot of salted water to a boil and set up a bowl of ice water. Add corn to the pot and cook for 2 minutes. Strain the corn and immediately plunge it into the bowl of ice water. Drain the corn and set aside.

In a medium bowl, toss the corn, mâche or arugula, blueberries, herbs and vinaigrette. Serve immediately. Makes 4 servings.

TODD COLEMAN

Garofalo

Katie Workman

Katie Workman is the founding editor in chief of Cookstr.com and author of The Mom 100 *(Workman Publishing, 2012). She writes about food and cooking for websites and magazines, including* The Huffington Post, AARP.com *and* The Wall Street Journal. *She is on the board of City Harvest, New York's leading food rescue nonprofit, and lives with her husband and two children in New York City.*

Garofalo

Big Batch Turkey Meat Sauce with Organic Penne
Garofalo

Recipes developed by Katie Workman

2 tablespoons olive oil, divided

1 pound ground turkey (don't buy the ultra-lean: use 93% lean/ 7% fat or 85/15)

1 pound fresh hot turkey sausage, removed from the casing

1 pound fresh sweet turkey sausage, removed from the casing

1½ cups chopped onions

3 shallots, finely chopped

1 tablespoon finely minced garlic

1 tablespoon dried oregano

2 teaspoons dried basil

Big glug or two of red or white wine, if you have a bottle open

4 cans (28 ounces each) crushed tomatoes, preferably in puree

½ teaspoon red pepper flakes (optional)

Kosher or coarse salt and freshly ground black pepper

1 16-ounce package Garofalo organic penne

Heat 1 tablespoon olive oil in a large stockpot over medium-high heat. Add ground turkey and turkey sausage meat and cook, stirring frequently and breaking up the meat until it's very crumbly and browned throughout, 4-6 minutes. Place the browned meat in a strainer and let the fat drain off.

Heat the remaining 1 tablespoon olive oil in the same pot over medium heat. Don't clean the pot! All those little browned bits of flavor from the meat will season the sauce. Add onions and shallots and cook, stirring frequently, until softened, about 5 minutes. Add garlic, oregano and basil, and cook, stirring, until you can smell the garlic and herbs, about 2 minutes. Add wine, if using, and cook, scraping up any bits stuck to the bottom of the pot, until the wine pretty much evaporates, about 1 minute.

Add tomatoes and red pepper flakes, if using, and stir to combine. Increase the heat to medium-high and let the tomato mixture come to a simmer, stirring it occasionally, for about 10 minutes. Add the browned turkey and sausage mixture, reduce the heat to medium-low and let simmer, stirring occasionally, until it's nicely thickened and the flavors have blended, about 20 minutes. Taste for seasoning, adding salt and black pepper as necessary. You won't need much; the sausages provide a whole lot of seasoning.

Bring a large pot of water to a boil over high heat. Add salt and let the water return to a boil. Add pasta and cook according to the package directions. Drain the pasta, return it to the pot and toss it with as much of the meat sauce as desired. Makes 6-8 servings, plus serious amounts of leftover sauce.

Sesame Noodles
Garofalo

Kosher or coarse salt (optional)

1 16-ounce package Garofalo spaghetti

SESAME SAUCE

1 2-inch piece peeled fresh ginger

3 garlic cloves

2 tablespoons light or dark brown sugar

⅓ cup creamy peanut butter

2 tablespoons rice vinegar or sherry vinegar

2 tablespoons regular or low-sodium soy sauce

½-1 teaspoon chili pepper sauce, such as Sriracha or Tabasco

3 tablespoons vegetable, peanut or canola oil

2 tablespoons Asian (dark) sesame oil, divided

GARNISH

2 scallions, thinly sliced; 1 table-spoon toasted sesame seeds; and/or fresh cilantro leaves

Prepare the sauce: Place ginger and garlic in a food processor or blender and run the machine until they are finely minced. Add brown sugar, peanut butter, vinegar, soy sauce, chili pepper sauce, vegetable oil and 1 tablespoon sesame oil. Process until smooth; reserve the sauce in the food processor.

Bring a large pot of water to a boil over high heat. Add salt and let the water return to a boil. Add spaghetti and cook according to the package directions until just tender. Set aside 1 cup of the noodle cooking water, then drain the noodles. Rinse them quickly with warm water and drain them again.

Add the reserved cup of cooking water to the sesame sauce and process to blend. Place the warm drained noodles in a large bowl and toss them with the remaining 1 tablespoon of sesame oil, then add the sesame sauce and mix everything until the noodles are well coated. Taste for seasoning, adding salt if necessary. Let the noodles cool to room temperature; they will absorb more sauce as they sit.

Garnish with scallions, sesame seeds and/or cilantro. Makes 8 side-dish servings.

Garofalo

Macaroni and Cheese
Garofalo

4 tablespoons unsalted butter

4 tablespoons all-purpose flour

½ teaspoon red pepper flakes (optional)

4½ cups 2% or whole milk

1 cup heavy (whipping) cream

5 cups coarsely grated flavorful cheese:
sharp Cheddar or Gruyère, or a mix

½ cup freshly grated
Parmesan cheese

4 teaspoons Dijon mustard

1½ teaspoons kosher or coarse salt

½ teaspoon freshly ground
black pepper

1½ packages (24 ounces)
Garofalo radiatore

PANKO TOPPING

3 tablespoons unsalted butter

3 cups panko bread crumbs

½ cup freshly grated
Parmesan cheese

Preheat oven to 400°F. Butter a shallow 4-quart baking dish.

Prepare the panko topping: Melt butter over low heat. Add panko and Parmesan; stir until well combined. Set aside.

Melt butter in a large heavy saucepan over medium heat. Whisk in flour and red pepper flakes. Cook, stirring, until flour is blond in color, about 4 minutes. Gradually whisk in milk. Increase heat to medium-high and let come to a simmer. Reduce heat to medium-low and simmer until it starts to thicken, about 5 minutes. Add cream, grated cheese, Parmesan, mustard, salt and pepper, stirring until smooth. Taste for seasoning.

Cook pasta until barely al dente (follow package directions but stop a minute or two before completely tender). Set aside 1 cup of the cooking water, then drain the pasta.

Whisk the reserved pasta cooking water into the cheese sauce. Add the pasta and stir to combine. Spoon into the prepared baking dish. Sprinkle with the panko topping.

Bake until golden and bubbling, 30-40 minutes. Let sit for a few minutes before serving. Makes 8-10 servings.

GEDIYON KIFLE

Marcus Samuelsson

Marcus Samuelsson is an international-
ally acclaimed chef who has thrilled
the food scene with a blend of culture
and artistic excellence. During his
tenure as executive chef at Aquavit,
he became the youngest person to
receive a three-star rating from the
New York Times. His newest restaurant, Red Rooster Harlem, celebrates
the roots of American cuisine. For
spice recipes and more, visit www.
MarcusSamuelsson.com.

THE
AUSTRALIAN LAMB
COMPANY INC.

Berbere-Crusted Rack of Lamb recipe on page 94.

THE
AUSTRALIAN LAMB
COMPANY INC.

Berbere-Crusted Rack of Lamb
The Lamb Cooperative

Recipe developed by Marcus Samuelsson

½ cup olive oil

1½ tablespoons coarsely
   chopped rosemary

1 large garlic clove, smashed

2 frenched Australian racks
   of lamb (1½ pounds each)

3 tablespoons berbere spice
   blend, divided

2 teaspoons Dijon mustard

2 teaspoons beaten egg yolk

¼ cup fine bread crumbs

2-3 tablespoons dry red wine, divided

½ cup chicken stock

2 tablespoons cold unsalted butter,
   cut into pieces

Combine oil, rosemary and garlic in a large zip-lock bag. Add lamb, then seal the bag, forcing out excess air. Marinate in the refrigerator for 8-24 hours, turning the bag several times.

Preheat oven to 400°F.

Stir together 1 tablespoon berbere, mustard, egg yolk and bread crumbs in a small bowl. Add 1-2 tablespoons wine, just enough to make a paste. Refrigerate until ready to use.

Remove the lamb from the marinade and pat dry; discard the marinade. Heat a large, heavy sauté pan over high heat until very hot. Reduce the heat to medium-high and brown the lamb, one rack at a time, about 3 minutes per side. Transfer, fat side up, to a large roasting pan.

Smear the berbere paste on the fat side of the lamb. Roast until a thermometer inserted in the center reads 135°F, for medium-rare, about 18-20 minutes. Transfer the lamb to a cutting board and let rest for 10 minutes.

While the lamb is roasting, toast the remaining 2 tablespoons berbere in a small, heavy saucepan over low heat, stirring constantly, until very fragrant, about 1 minute. Add chicken stock and 1 tablespoon wine and bring to a boil, then boil until reduced to the consistency of a sauce. Remove from the heat and whisk in the butter bit by bit until incorporated.

Cut the lamb into chops and serve the sauce on the side. Makes 6-8 servings.

Recipes adapted with permission from The Soul of a New Cuisine, *by Marcus Samuelsson (Wiley, 2006).*

Berbere-Crusted Rack of Lamb photo on page 93.

Lamb Curry
The Lamb Cooperative

Recipe developed by Marcus Samuelsson

1 cup unsalted butter

4 medium red onions,
   sliced

4 3-inch pieces ginger,
   peeled and grated

12 garlic cloves, crushed

4 bird's-eye chilies, seeds
   and ribs removed,
   finely chopped

4 teaspoons paprika

4 teaspoons ground
   coriander

8 cardamom pods

4 bay leaves

4 cinnamon sticks

½ teaspoon
   powdered saffron

2 teaspoons
   ground turmeric

2 teaspoons black
   peppercorns

4 pounds Australian
   boneless leg of lamb,
   cut into 2-inch cubes

3 cups chopped fresh
   or canned tomatoes

2 cups coconut milk

4 cups water, divided

6 large Yukon Gold
   potatoes (1½ pounds
   total), peeled and cut
   in half

4 cups okra in
   2-inch pieces

2 cups plain yogurt

Cooked rice, for serving

Melt butter in a large sauté pan over medium heat. Stir in onions, ginger, garlic and chilies, and sauté until the onions are translucent, about 10 minutes. Add paprika, coriander, cardamom, bay leaves, cinnamon sticks, saffron, turmeric and peppercorns, and cook, stirring constantly, until fragrant, about 30 seconds.

Add lamb and tomatoes. Simmer, uncovered, for 5 minutes. Stir in coconut milk and 2 cups of the water and bring to a simmer, then reduce the heat to low and simmer gently, uncovered, for 1½ hours.

Add the remaining 2 cups water and simmer, uncovered, for 40 minutes. Add potatoes, cover, and simmer until the meat is tender, about 40 minutes longer.

Add okra and cook for 10 minutes, or until tender. Remove from the heat, remove bay leaves and stir in yogurt 1 tablespoon at a time.

Serve with rice. Makes 12-16 servings.

THE
AUSTRALIAN LAMB
COMPANY INC.

Herb-Crusted Loin Lamb Chops with Tomato Mint Salad
The Lamb Cooperative

8 Australian loin lamb chops
1-2 tablespoons Dijon or coarse-grain mustard
Olive oil
Lemon wedges

HERB CRUST
½ cup fresh bread crumbs or diced baguette
4 large fresh basil leaves
1 tablespoon grated Parmesan cheese
1 tablespoon pine nuts (optional)

TOMATO MINT SALAD
1 pint cherry tomatoes, halved
8-10 pitted green olives, sliced
¼ cup sliced fresh mint leaves
1 tablespoon wine vinegar
Salt and freshly ground
   pepper to taste

Prepare the crust: Place all ingredients in a small blender (or coffee grinder in small batches) and process to combine. Transfer to a plate.

Cover lamb chops with mustard. Place the chops on the crust mixture and press firmly, coating both sides. Cover with plastic and refrigerate for 10 minutes to set the crust.

Prepare the salad: Combine all ingredients and set aside.

Heat a nonstick or cast-iron skillet to medium and add enough oil to coat. Add the chops and cook for 3-4 minutes on each side, or until cooked to taste (suggested internal temperature of 145°F) and the crust is crisp and browned.

Serve with the salad and lemon wedges. A green salad and the rest of the baguette are the perfect match for this dish. Makes 4 servings.

Rebecca Spence

Costco member Rebecca Spence's recipe had been six years in the making when she entered the 2011 Foster Farms Fresh Chicken Cooking Contest. Spence spent years experimenting with ingredients until she hit upon her winning recipe— which netted her $10,000 and a one-year supply of Foster Farms fresh chicken. For more about Foster Farms' Fresh Chicken Cooking Contest, visit www.fosterfarms.com/cookingcontest.

ED ANDERSON

Crispy Orange Chicken with Fennel, Avocado and Orange Salad

Foster Farms

Recipe developed by Rebecca Spence

1 tablespoon orange juice
1 tablespoon Champagne vinegar (or white wine vinegar)
2 teaspoons sugar
Grated zest from 2 large navel oranges (reserve 1 orange), divided
2 teaspoons salt, divided
¾ teaspoon freshly ground black pepper, divided
2 tablespoons extra-virgin olive oil
1 large fennel bulb, trimmed

1 large avocado
1 serrano chile
½ cup flour
2 eggs
2 cups panko bread crumbs
½ cup peanut oil
1-1½ pounds Foster Farms fresh boneless, skinless chicken breasts, each sliced horizontally into 2 fillets

In a large bowl, whisk together orange juice, vinegar, sugar, 1 teaspoon orange zest, ½ teaspoon salt and ¼ teaspoon black pepper. Slowly whisk in olive oil. Set aside.

Cut white pith away from the reserved zested orange; cut orange into small cubes. Chop fennel into small cubes. Peel avocado, remove pit and chop into small cubes. Cut chile in half lengthwise, remove and discard seeds, and finely mince. Place the orange pieces, fennel, avocado and chile in the bowl with the dressing; toss gently and refrigerate while preparing the chicken.

Preheat oven to 200°F. In a shallow bowl, mix flour with the remaining salt and pepper. In a second shallow bowl, beat eggs well with a fork. Place panko in a third shallow bowl and stir in the remaining orange zest.

In a large skillet over medium-high heat, warm peanut oil. Dredge each piece of chicken in the flour mixture, then dip in the egg and coat with panko-orange mixture. Place the coated chicken in the hot oil and sauté for about 5 minutes on each side, or until golden brown and cooked through. Remove with tongs and place on a rack over a cookie sheet in the oven to keep warm.

Serve with the salad. Makes 4 servings.

Asian Chicken Lettuce Wraps

Foster Farms

3 tablespoons hoisin sauce
1 tablespoon rice vinegar
1 tablespoon low-sodium soy sauce
1½ teaspoons dark brown sugar
¼ teaspoon hot chili sauce
1¾ teaspoons sesame oil, divided
1 tablespoon vegetable oil
3 green onions, chopped
1 teaspoon chopped garlic

½ teaspoon minced fresh ginger
½ red bell pepper, chopped
8 ounces mushrooms, chopped
1 16-ounce pouch Kirkland Signature/Foster Farms Grilled Chicken Breast Strips, chopped
½ large head of iceberg lettuce, cored and quartered, leaves separated (or 8 lettuce leaves)

In a small bowl, stir together hoisin sauce, vinegar, soy sauce, brown sugar, chili sauce and ¼ teaspoon sesame oil. Set aside.

Heat vegetable oil and 1½ teaspoons sesame oil in a skillet over medium-high heat. Add green onions, garlic and ginger; cook for 2 minutes, or until fragrant. Add bell pepper and mushrooms; cook for 2 minutes. Add chicken and heat thoroughly, about 2 minutes. Add the sauce mixture to the skillet, tossing to coat.

Spoon the chicken mixture into the lettuce leaves. Makes 4 servings.

Myra Goodman

Myra Goodman and her husband, Drew, founded Earthbound Farm in their Carmel Valley, California, backyard 28 years ago. Myra's cooking is inspired by the fresh, flavorful and healthy harvest of their organic farm, which led her to establish one of the country's first certified organic kitchens. Her latest cookbook is The Earthbound Cook: 250 Recipes for Delicious Food and a Healthy Planet *(Workman Publishing, 2010).*

Baby Kale and Baby Spinach Salad with Carrots, Cranberries and Almonds
Earthbound Farm

Recipes developed by Myra Goodman

4 cups Earthbound Farm organic mixed baby kales (or substitute Earthbound Farm organic spring mix)

4 cups Earthbound Farm organic baby spinach

¼ cup peeled and shredded Earthbound Farm organic carrots

¼ cup dried cranberries

¼ cup toasted almonds, chopped

VINAIGRETTE

2 tablespoons orange juice

2 tablespoons tamari or soy sauce

2 tablespoons golden balsamic vinegar

1 teaspoon grated fresh ginger

3 tablespoons canola oil

3 tablespoons toasted sesame oil

Salt and freshly ground pepper to taste

Prepare the vinaigrette: Combine orange juice, tamari sauce, vinegar and ginger in a mixing bowl. In a measuring cup, combine both oils and drizzle into the orange juice-vinegar mixture, whisking to combine. Season with salt and pepper. (Vinaigrette can be refrigerated, covered, for up to 3 weeks.)

Place baby kales, spinach, carrots, cranberries and almonds in a large mixing bowl. Dress with half of the vinaigrette and toss, adding more vinaigrette if desired. Serve immediately. Serves 6 as a side salad.

Mixed Baby Kales and Farro Salad with Mustard Vinaigrette
Earthbound Farm

1½ cups uncooked farro

1 cup cherry tomatoes, cut in half

4½ cups Earthbound Farm organic mixed baby kales, coarsely chopped

¾ cup Earthbound Farm organic carrots, peeled and grated

1 cup corn kernels, fresh or frozen

MUSTARD VINAIGRETTE

2 tablespoons lemon juice

1 tablespoon Dijon mustard

1 tablespoon tamari or soy sauce

2 teaspoons minced shallot

1 teaspoon minced garlic

2 teaspoons chopped fresh parsley

½ cup extra-virgin olive oil

¾ teaspoon salt

Freshly ground black pepper to taste

Prepare the vinaigrette: Combine lemon juice, mustard, tamari sauce, shallot, garlic and parsley in a large bowl. Slowly drizzle the oil into the mixture while whisking. Season with salt and pepper.

Bring 6 cups of water to a boil in a large covered saucepan over high heat. Add a pinch of salt and the farro, and return to a boil. Then reduce the heat to medium-low and cook, stirring occasionally, until the farro is puffed and slightly chewy, 20-30 minutes. (Do not overcook, or the farro will be mushy.)

Drain the farro immediately, and rinse it under cold running water until cool. Drain again and transfer to a large bowl. Add cherry tomatoes, baby kales, carrots and corn. Stir in vinaigrette, and adjust the seasoning if desired. Serve immediately. Serves 8 as a side salad.

MICHAEL FRIEDMAN

Joy Wilson

Joy Wilson's father taught her how to bake a pie when she was 6 years old, and she's been in the kitchen ever since. Wilson is a professional baker, and the voice behind the blog Joy the Baker (joythebaker.com). She is the author of Joy the Baker Cookbook (Hyperion, 2012) and is a curator of all things sweet.

Puratos
Reliable partners in innovation

Double Chocolate Chunk Trifle

Kirkland Signature/Puratos

Recipes developed by Joy Wilson

1 3.9-ounce package instant chocolate pudding mix

¾ cup cold milk

1 14-ounce can sweetened condensed milk

6 Kirkland Signature double chocolate or vanilla chocolate chunk muffins

4 cups fresh berries

WHIPPED CREAM

3 cups heavy cream

½ cup confectioners' sugar

1 tablespoon pure vanilla extract

Prepare the whipped cream: Using an electric stand mixer fitted with a whisk attachment, combine
cream, confectioners' sugar and vanilla. Whip on medium speed until soft peaks form. Set aside.

Place pudding mix in a medium bowl. Slowly whisk in cold milk and sweetened condensed milk, whisking until smooth. With a spatula, fold in 1 cup of whipped cream until no streaks remain. Set aside.

Cut muffins into bite-size pieces. Cut any large berries into bite-size pieces.

Place half of the muffin pieces in an even layer in a large trifle bowl or glass serving bowl. Layer with half of the pudding mixture and then half of the whipped cream and berries. Repeat the layering with the remaining muffin chunks, pudding, whipped cream and berries.

Cover with plastic wrap and chill in the refrigerator for at least 6 hours and up to 24 hours. Makes 10 servings.

Quick Pull-Apart Danish Apple Cheesecakes

Kirkland Signature/Puratos

4 Fuji apples, peeled, cored and sliced thin

1 tablespoon lemon juice

3 tablespoons light brown sugar

1 teaspoon ground cinnamon

1 teaspoon cornstarch

Pinch of ground allspice

Pinch of salt

2 tablespoons unsalted butter, cut into small cubes

6 Kirkland Signature cheese pull-apart Danish pastries

Preheat oven to 400°F. Line a baking sheet with parchment paper.

Spread sliced apples across the baking sheet. Sprinkle with lemon juice. Sprinkle with brown sugar, cinnamon, cornstarch, allspice and salt. Toss with your fingers. Top with butter cubes.

Bake on the center oven rack for 15-25 minutes, or until golden and bubbly. Let cool slightly, then top each Danish with warm apples and serve immediately. Makes 6 servings.

Strawberry Coconut Croissant Bread Pudding
Kirkland Signature/Puratos

10 Kirkland Signature butter croissants
1 cup coarsely chopped fresh strawberries
1 cup sweetened shredded coconut, toasted
8 large eggs
1 cup granulated sugar

¼ cup packed light brown sugar
¼ teaspoon salt
2 cups heavy cream
1 14-ounce can coconut milk
1 tablespoon pure vanilla extract

Lightly butter a 13-by-9-inch baking pan.

Slice croissants in half horizontally. Reserve the top half of 8 croissants. Tear the remaining croissants into bite-size pieces.

Place the torn croissant pieces in the prepared pan. Top with strawberries and coconut. Use your fingers to toss the mixture together. Arrange the 8 croissant halves on top.

In a large bowl, whisk eggs until thoroughly combined. Whisk in sugars and salt. Then gradually whisk in cream, coconut milk and vanilla.

Pour the wet ingredients over the croissant mixture. Press the croissants into the liquid to ensure that all the bread pieces are moistened. Cover with plastic wrap and refrigerate for 1-3 hours.

When ready to bake, preheat oven to 350°F. Bring a kettle of water to a boil. Place a pie dish on the lower oven rack and fill halfway with boiling water.

Uncover the chilled bread pudding and place on the center oven rack above the pie dish. Bake until set, about 40-45 minutes. Check after 30 minutes, and if the pudding is browning too much, cover with foil.

Serve warm or at room temperature. Makes 8-10 servings.

JAN COBB

Joy Bauer

Joy Bauer, MS, RD, CDN, is one of the nation's leading health authorities. She is the nutrition and health expert for NBC's Today show, a monthly columnist for Woman's Day magazine and the exclusive nutritionist for the New York City Ballet. Bauer is the creator of JoyBauer.com and the author of several best-selling books, including Joy Bauer's Food Cures (Rodale, 2011).

DELANO FARMS

Curried Chicken Salad with Grapes recipe on page 104.

Curried Chicken Salad with Grapes
Quick & Easy

Delano Farms

Recipes developed by Joy Bauer

5 ounces cooked chicken breast, shredded or chopped (canned or fresh)

1 tablespoon reduced-fat mayonnaise

1 teaspoon curry powder

½ cup sliced Delano Farms green seedless grapes (see note)

3-4 cups salad greens, for serving

In a bowl, mash chicken. Gently mix with mayonnaise, curry powder and grapes.

To serve, scoop the chicken salad on top of the salad greens. Makes 1 serving.

Nutritional information: 300 calories, 46 g protein, 22 g carbohydrates, 5 g fat, 105 mg cholesterol, 4 g fiber, 280 mg sodium, 12 g sugar.

Note: Grapes of any color can be used in these recipes.

Curried Chicken Salad with Grapes photo on page 103.

PB-Grape Breakfast Pocket
Quick & Easy

Delano Farms

1 whole-grain pita bread, toasted

2 tablespoons natural peanut butter

½ cup sliced Delano Farms black seedless grapes

Cut a slit in the pita to create a pocket.

Spread peanut butter on the inside of the pocket and stuff with the grapes. Seal it up and bite in! Makes 1 serving.

Nutritional information: 380 calories, 16 g protein, 48 g carbohydrates, 17 g fat, 0 mg cholesterol, 7 g fiber, 310 mg sodium, 14 g sugar.

Protein Pancake with Sliced Grapes
Delano Farms

½ cup quick-cooking oats

4 egg whites

½ teaspoon vanilla extract

1 teaspoon sugar

½ cup sliced Delano Farms red seedless grapes

1 teaspoon maple syrup (optional)

Generously coat a skillet with oil spray and preheat over medium heat. In a small bowl, whip together oats, egg whites, vanilla and sugar. Pour the mixture into the skillet and cook for 2-3 minutes, or until golden brown, on each side.

Transfer the pancake to a plate. Top with grapes and drizzle with maple syrup, or toss grapes with syrup. Makes 1 serving.

Tip: For a moister pancake, cover the skillet with a lid while the pancake is cooking.

Nutritional information: 285 calories, 20 g protein, 46 g carbohydrates, 3 g fat, 0 mg cholesterol, 4 g fiber, 220 mg sodium, 17 g sugar.

BILL NYGARD

Ree Drummond

Ree Drummond is the best-selling author of two cookbooks, including her latest, The Pioneer Woman Cooks (William Morrow Cookbooks, 2012). Her website, thepioneerwoman.com, was founded in 2006 and showcases her cooking, photography and stories about country life. Her cooking show, The Pioneer Woman, premiered on Food Network in 2011. She lives on a working cattle ranch in Oklahoma with her husband and four children.

Spicy Chili Pork Ree-yubs

JBS/Swift Premium

Recipes developed by Ree Drummond

3 pounds Swift Premium St. Louis-style pork ribs

Vegetable oil

2 tablespoons chili powder

1 tablespoon garlic salt

1 tablespoon ground cumin

¼ cup brown sugar

1 tablespoon ground black pepper

1 teaspoon cayenne pepper

Your favorite barbecue sauce (optional)

Lay the ribs on a large piece of aluminum foil and rub with oil.

Combine chili powder, garlic salt, cumin, sugar, black pepper and cayenne. Rub the mixture into the ribs until fully coated.

Wrap the foil around the ribs (use more foil if necessary to cover tightly). Refrigerate for at least 2 hours and up to overnight. Cook the ribs using one of the following methods:

Grill and oven method: Preheat the grill to high. Preheat oven to 335°F. Remove the foil and set aside. Grill the ribs until browned, about 6-7 minutes per side. Transfer the ribs to a sheet pan and wrap in the foil again. Cook in the oven for 2 hours, or until the meat is tender. If you're using barbecue sauce, remove the foil, coat the ribs with sauce and return to the oven for 10-15 minutes.

Oven method: Preheat oven to 335°F. Place the ribs on a sheet pan and cook in the oven for 2 hours, or until the meat is tender. If you're using barbecue sauce, remove the foil, coat the ribs with sauce and return to the oven for 10-15 minutes.

Grill method: Preheat the grill to high. Remove the foil and set aside. Grill the ribs until browned, about 6-7 minutes per side. Wrap the ribs in foil again. Turn off a portion of the burners, turn the heat to 335-350°F and place the ribs on the cooler side of the grill. Cook for an additional 1½-2 hours, or until the meat is tender. If you're using barbecue sauce, remove the ribs from the foil, coat them with sauce and grill for 5-10 minutes more.

Slice between each rib and serve. Makes 2-3 servings.

Whiskey Chicken Thighs with Pasta and Mushrooms

Pilgrim's/Gold Kist Farms

1½ pounds baby portobellos or similar mushrooms, thickly sliced

4 tablespoons olive oil, divided

Kosher salt

Black pepper

2 tablespoons butter

1 pound Gold Kist boneless, skinless chicken thighs

1 large onion, peeled and sliced

1 cup dry white wine

¾ cup classic American whiskey (such as Jack Daniel's)

1 cup chicken broth

1 cup heavy cream

12 ounces mostaccioli or penne, cooked al dente

Preheat oven to 375°F.

Spread mushrooms on a baking sheet. Drizzle with 2 tablespoons olive oil, then sprinkle with salt and pepper to taste. Roast for 20-25 minutes, or until golden brown. Set aside.

In a large skillet or Dutch oven, heat 2 tablespoons olive oil and butter over medium heat. Add chicken thighs and cook on both sides until browned, about 5 minutes total. Remove the chicken to a plate.

Add onion to the pan and sauté for 2-3 minutes, or until it begins to turn translucent. Pour in wine and whiskey, bring the liquid to a boil and let it bubble for 1-2 minutes. Add chicken broth.

Return the chicken to the pan, reduce the heat to low and simmer for 20-25 minutes. At the end, stir in cream. Add the mushrooms and salt and pepper to taste. Simmer until the sauce thickens.

Toss in the cooked pasta, adding a little hot pasta water if the sauce needs thinning. Adjust the seasonings as desired and serve. Makes 6 servings.

Matt Scialabba and Melissa Pellegrino

Matt Scialabba and Melissa Pellegrino are a husband-and-wife cooking and writing team who met while studying in Italy, where they learned the secrets of authentic regional cuisine. They are authors of The Southern Italian Farmer's Table *(Lyons Press, 2012; www.theitalian farmerstable.com) and chef/owners of Bufalina in Guilford, Connecticut, which specializes in wood-fired pizza.*

Mixed Mushroom Pizza with Sausage and Fontina

Premio

Recipes developed by Matt Scialabba and Melissa Pellegrino

1 pound pizza dough, at room temperature

Unbleached all-purpose flour

8 ounces mixed mushrooms (such as crimini, shiitake and hen of the woods), thinly sliced

1 teaspoon finely chopped fresh rosemary

Kosher salt and freshly ground black pepper

1 tablespoon extra-virgin olive oil

1 cup shredded Fontina cheese

2 links (about ½ pound) Premio hot Italian sausage, casings removed and cut into small pieces

At least 30 minutes before baking, position a rack in the bottom third of the oven; if using a pizza stone, set it on the rack. (If you don't have a stone, use a heavy-duty 18-by-13-inch baking sheet lightly coated with olive oil.) Heat the oven to 500°F. If using a pizza stone, dust a pizza peel with flour.

On a lightly floured surface, stretch the dough into a rough circle about 12 inches in diameter and ⅛ inch thick. Transfer the stretched dough to the prepared pizza peel or baking sheet.

In a large bowl, toss together mushrooms, rosemary, a pinch of salt and a few grinds of fresh pepper. Add oil and toss well to coat the mushrooms. Spread the mushroom mixture over the dough, leaving a ½-inch border. Sprinkle cheese evenly over the dough and then evenly disperse the sausage.

If using a baking sheet, put it on the oven rack. If using a pizza stone, slide the pizza off the peel and onto the heated stone. Bake until the crust is nicely browned and crisp and the cheese is bubbly, about 12-15 minutes on a pizza stone or 15-20 minutes on a baking sheet. Transfer the pizza to a cutting board and let stand for 1-2 minutes before cutting. Makes 4 appetizer or 2 entrée servings.

Braised Chicken Legs with Sausage, Beans and Cipolline Onions

Premio

4 chicken legs (about 2½ pounds)

Kosher salt and freshly ground black pepper

2 tablespoons extra-virgin olive oil, divided

1 pound Premio mild Italian sausages, cut into 2-inch pieces

¾ pound small cipolline onions, peeled

1 carrot, peeled and finely chopped

1 celery stalk, finely chopped

½ cup dry white wine

1½ cups low-sodium chicken broth

1 rosemary sprig

1 15-ounce can cannellini beans, drained and rinsed

Lightly season chicken legs all over with salt and pepper.

Heat 1 tablespoon oil in a 12-inch straight-sided skillet over medium-high heat. Add sausage and cook until browned all over, 5-7 minutes. Transfer to a plate.

Add the chicken and cook until deep golden brown, 2-3 minutes. Flip the chicken over and continue cooking until browned, about 3 minutes. Transfer to the plate with the sausage.

Pour off all but a thin layer of fat from the pan and add the remaining tablespoon of oil. Add onions, carrot, celery and a pinch of salt and cook until fragrant, 3-4 minutes. Add wine to the pan, scrape up any browned bits with a wooden spoon and cook until reduced by half. Add chicken broth and bring to a boil. Return the chicken legs and sausage to the pan, along with the rosemary. Cover the pan, reduce the heat to maintain a gentle simmer and cook for 25 minutes. Add beans and continue cooking, covered, until the chicken is fork tender, 20-25 minutes more. Makes 4 servings.

MICHELLE VAN VLIET

Clifford A. Wright

Clifford A. Wright is the author of 13 cookbooks, including A Mediterranean Feast (William Morrow, 1999), which won the James Beard/KitchenAid Cookbook of the Year award and the James Beard Award for the Best Writing on Food in 2000. Wright's articles on food and cuisine have appeared in Gourmet, Bon Appétit, Saveur and other magazines. For more information, visit www.cliffordawright.com.

Breakfast Strata
Tarantino

Recipes developed by Clifford A. Wright

1 cup small broccoli florets

½ pound Tarantino breakfast sausages, casings removed, crumbled

1 pound white button mushrooms, stems removed, caps thinly sliced

Freshly ground black pepper

½ pound white loaf bread, sliced ½ inch thick, crusts removed

Salt

1½ cups milk

½ pound ricotta cheese, at room temperature

¼ cup unbleached all-purpose flour

1 tablespoon baking powder

9 large eggs

1½ pounds freshly grated or shredded Monterey Jack cheese

¼ pound freshly grated or shredded sharp Cheddar cheese

2 cups chopped scallions, green part only

Lightly butter a 15-by-10-inch baking casserole or roasting pan.

Bring a saucepan of water to a boil over high heat. Add broccoli florets and cook until slightly tender, about 4 minutes. Drain and set aside.

In a skillet, cook sausage over medium heat, breaking it up with a wooden spoon, until it is brown, about 6 minutes. Add mushrooms to the skillet and cook, stirring frequently, until softened, about 4 minutes. Season to taste with pepper. Remove from the heat and cool slightly.

Toast bread slices until they are golden, then sprinkle them with salt. Line the baking casserole with the toast.

In a large bowl, using an electric mixer, beat milk and ricotta until well blended. Whisk in flour, baking powder and ½ teaspoon salt. Add eggs one at a time, whisking until each is fully incorporated. Stir in the sausage-and-mushroom mixture, cheeses, broccoli and scallions. Pour over the toasts. Cover tightly with plastic wrap and refrigerate overnight.

Remove the casserole from the refrigerator 30 minutes before baking. Preheat oven to 350°F.

Uncover the casserole and bake until the strata is golden brown on top and the sides are set but the center jiggles slightly, about 1 hour. Cool for 5-10 minutes before serving. Makes 8-10 servings.

Adapted with permission from Bake Until Bubbly, *by Clifford A. Wright (Wiley, 2008).*

Grilled Skewers of Sausage, Orange and Bay Leaf
Tarantino

10 bay leaves

10 6- to 8-inch wooden skewers, soaked in water for 60 minutes

1½ pounds Tarantino mild Italian sausage links, cut into 1-inch chunks

1 small onion, quartered and separated

1 Valencia (juice) orange, cut in chunks the same size as the sausage

Extra-virgin olive oil, for drizzling

Prepare a hot charcoal fire or preheat a gas grill on high.

Put bay leaves into some tepid water while you work so they soften.

On the skewers, thread sausage, onion, bay leaf, sausage, orange and sausage, in that order.

Drizzle the food with oil and grill until it is blackening, about 20 minutes, turning occasionally. Serve immediately. Makes 2-4 servings.

Baked Angel Hair Pasta with Sausages and Smooth Tomato and Artichoke Sauce
Tarantino

2 pounds (about 8 links) Tarantino mild Italian sausages

4 bay leaves

½ cup extra-virgin olive oil

1 small onion, finely chopped

1 celery stalk, finely chopped

¼ cup finely chopped fresh parsley

3 large garlic cloves, finely chopped

3 large ripe tomatoes (about 1½ pounds), peeled, seeded and finely chopped, or 1 28-ounce can whole tomatoes

½ red bell pepper, seeded and finely chopped

5 marinated or fresh artichoke hearts, chopped

Salt and freshly ground pepper

1 pound angel hair pasta (capellini)

Freshly grated Parmesan cheese, for garnish

Preheat oven to 350°F. Lightly oil a 12-by-9-by-2-inch baking casserole. Place sausages in the casserole. Stick bay leaves between some sausages. Place the casserole in the oven until the sausages are fully cooked, about 30 minutes.

Remove the sausages from the casserole and set aside.

In a skillet, heat oil over medium heat. Add onion, celery, parsley and garlic, and cook, stirring frequently, until softened, about 6 minutes. Add tomatoes, bell pepper and artichoke hearts. Season to taste with salt and pepper. Reduce the heat to low, cover and cook, stirring occasionally, until denser, about 50 minutes. Pass the sauce through a strainer and set aside.

Bring a large pot of salted water to a vigorous boil. Add pasta and boil until half-cooked (follow the package instructions), about 1½ minutes. Drain and toss the pasta with the sauce.

Arrange the pasta in the empty casserole that the sausages were cooked in and place the sausages in rows on top. Bake until the top of the pasta begins to get a little crunchy, 20-25 minutes. Sprinkle Parmesan liberally over the casserole and serve. Makes 4-6 servings.

Adapted with permission from Bake Until Bubbly, *by Clifford A. Wright (Wiley).*

PLUME DE VEAU
The First Name in Veal

ANTHONYGARITOOFJACKSTUDIOS

David Burke

Blurring the lines between inventor, chef and entrepreneur, David Burke (www.davidburke.com) is one of the pioneers in American cooking today. He is the innovator behind flavor-transfer spice sheets and more, his fascination with ingredients fueling a career marked by creativity and acclaim. He's written two books and publishes his own quarterly magazine, available in any of his restaurants.

Veal Rib Chops with Watercress Sauce recipe on page 114.

Veal Rib Chops
with Watercress Sauce

Plume De Veau

Recipes developed by David Burke

2 bunches of watercress

4 tablespoons clarified butter
   or olive oil

4 Plume De Veau veal rib chops

Coarse or kosher salt and freshly
   ground pepper

1 cup light chicken stock or
   canned chicken broth

Juice of 1 lemon

4 tablespoons butter, divided

½ cup minced carrots

Risotto or mashed potatoes,
   for serving

Blanch watercress in boiling salted water for 2 minutes. Drain. Place watercress in a food processor and puree. Set aside.

Preheat oven to 400°F.

Heat clarified butter over medium-high heat in a large sauté pan, preferably nonstick. Season chops with salt and pepper to taste. Sauté for about 3 minutes on each side, or until lightly browned.

Place the chops on a baking sheet and transfer to the oven. Cook for an additional 6-8 minutes.

While the chops roast, drain the fat from the sauté pan. Add stock or broth and lemon juice and cook until reduced by half.

Add the watercress puree and 2 tablespoons butter to the pan and cook for an additional minute, stirring to combine. Correct the seasoning.

Heat 2 tablespoons butter in a small saucepan over medium-high heat. Add carrots and cook, stirring, for 1-2 minutes, or until tender. Season to taste. Set aside.

Place risotto or mashed potatoes on 4 plates. Place 1 chop on top of each serving. Spoon watercress sauce around the perimeter of each plate. Mound carrots on top of each chop. Makes 4 servings.

Veal Rib Chops with Watercress Sauce photo on page 113.

Veal Scallopini Marsala

Plume De Veau

1 cup flour

1 tablespoon garlic powder

1 tablespoon freshly ground pepper

1 tablespoon coarse or kosher salt

1 pound Plume De Veau veal scallopini

4 tablespoons olive oil, divided

1 cup sliced mushrooms (any type)

1 cup Marsala wine

1 cup chicken stock

1 tablespoon chopped fresh
   Italian parsley

In a shallow dish, mix together flour, garlic powder, pepper and salt.

Dredge veal in the seasoned flour mix, shaking off excess flour from each piece.

Warm 2 tablespoons oil in a large nonstick frying pan over medium-high heat. Sauté the veal for 30-60 seconds per side, turning only once when golden brown. When finished, keep the veal warm on a covered platter.

Add 2 tablespoons oil to the pan over medium-high heat. Add mushrooms and sauté until lightly browned, 3-4 minutes.

Deglaze the pan with Marsala and chicken stock. Cook until reduced by half. If the sauce gets too thick, add more Marsala. Season to taste with salt and pepper.

Serve the scallopini with the sauce and mushrooms spooned over the top. Sprinkle each plate with chopped parsley. Makes 4 servings.

Tip: Serve with pasta or mashed potatoes, with Marsala sauce spooned over them as well.

Osso Buco with Pasta
Plume De Veau

4 Plume De Veau veal shanks

Coarse or kosher salt and freshly ground pepper

1 tablespoon olive oil

1 carrot, minced

1 celery stalk, minced

1 small onion, minced

4 sprigs fresh rosemary or ½ teaspoon crushed dried rosemary

2 quarts brown stock or canned beef broth

PASTA

2 tablespoons butter

¼ cup diced yellow squash

¼ cup diced zucchini

1 small carrot, blanched until tender (2-3 minutes) and diced

Coarse or kosher salt and freshly ground pepper

1 cup orecchiette pasta, or small pasta shells, cooked al dente

GARNISH

2 lemons, each cut into 6 sections

4 sprigs fresh rosemary

1 tablespoon grated lemon zest

Preheat oven to 350°F. Season veal shanks with salt and pepper to taste. Heat oil over medium-high heat in an ovenproof casserole or Dutch oven. Sauté the veal shanks, turning once or twice, until they are lightly browned. Add carrot, celery and onion. Stir and brown the meat and vegetables for an additional 5 minutes. Stir in rosemary.

Add stock or broth. Cover and bring the sauce to a simmer. Transfer the pot to the oven and braise for 1½-2 hours, or until the veal is tender. Remove the veal shanks from the pot and keep warm. Strain the sauce and cook until reduced to approximately 1½ cups.

Prepare the pasta: Heat butter in a large sauté pan over medium-high heat. Add squash, zucchini and carrot, and sauté for 2 minutes. Season to taste with salt and pepper. Add cooked pasta and toss to combine.

To serve, make a pool of sauce in the center of each of 4 dinner plates. Spoon the vegetable-pasta mixture into the center of the sauce. Set a veal shank on top. Place 3 lemon sections beside each shank. Top the veal with rosemary and scatter lemon zest around the plates. Makes 4 servings.

Melissa d'Arabian

Melissa d'Arabian is host of Food Network's daytime cooking series Ten Dollar Dinners *and Cooking Channel's* Drop 5 Lbs with Good Housekeeping. *D'Arabian is the season-five winner of* The Next Food Network Star *and has also appeared on Food Network's* The Best Thing I Ever Ate *and* Food Network Challenge. *She lives with her husband, Philippe, and their four young daughters in San Diego.*

BEN FINK

Spinach Salad with Blue Cheese and Pears
First Fruits

Recipes developed by Melissa d'Arabian

⅓ cup pecan halves

2 pinches of kosher salt, divided

½ small red onion, thinly sliced

1 First Fruits pear, cored and thinly sliced

1 teaspoon fresh lemon juice

3 cups baby spinach

¼ cup crumbled blue cheese

1 tablespoon white wine vinegar

⅛ teaspoon ground black pepper

2 tablespoons olive oil

Preheat oven to 375°F.

Place pecans on a rimmed baking sheet and roast until fragrant and toasted, 5-7 minutes. Transfer to a large plate, sprinkle with a pinch of salt and set aside.

Prepare an ice-water bath in a small bowl. Submerge onion slices and set aside for 10 minutes. Drain, place the onion on a paper towel and set aside.

Place pear slices in a large salad bowl and gently toss with lemon juice. Add spinach, cheese and onion.

Whisk vinegar, a pinch of salt and pepper together in a small bowl. Whisk in oil and then pour over the spinach. Toss together, sprinkle the pecans over the top and serve. Makes 4 servings.

Recipes adapted from the book Ten Dollar Dinners, *by Melissa d'Arabian. Copyright © 2012 by Melissa d'Arabian. Published by Clarkson Potter, a division of Random House, Inc.*

Apple-Carrot Mini Muffins
First Fruits

½ cup all-purpose flour

½ cup whole-wheat flour

½ cup bran flake cereal

¼ cup ground flax seeds

2 tablespoons wheat germ

1 teaspoon baking powder

1 teaspoon baking soda

1 teaspoon ground cinnamon

Pinch of kosher salt

1 large egg

¼ cup packed light brown sugar, plus more for topping

2 tablespoons olive oil

1 teaspoon vanilla extract

⅔ cup plus 1 tablespoon whole milk

¾ cup grated carrots (see note)

½ cup finely chopped First Fruits apple and/or pear

Preheat oven to 350°F. Spray a 24-cup mini muffin pan with nonstick spray or line with mini muffin liners.

Whisk all-purpose flour, whole-wheat flour, bran flakes, flax seeds, wheat germ, baking powder, baking soda, cinnamon and salt together in a large bowl.

Whisk egg and sugar together in a medium bowl. Mix in oil and vanilla, then whisk in milk. Use a wooden spoon to stir in carrots and apple, then pour the egg mixture over the flour mixture. Stir just until combined.

Divide the batter among the prepared muffin cups, filling each one about ¾ full. If you'd like, sprinkle a little sugar over each muffin. Bake until the centers of the muffins spring back to light pressure, 10-15 minutes. Remove from the oven and cool for a few minutes in the pan before transferring to a rack to cool completely. Makes 24 mini muffins.

Note: Other vegetables such as spinach or zucchini can be used.

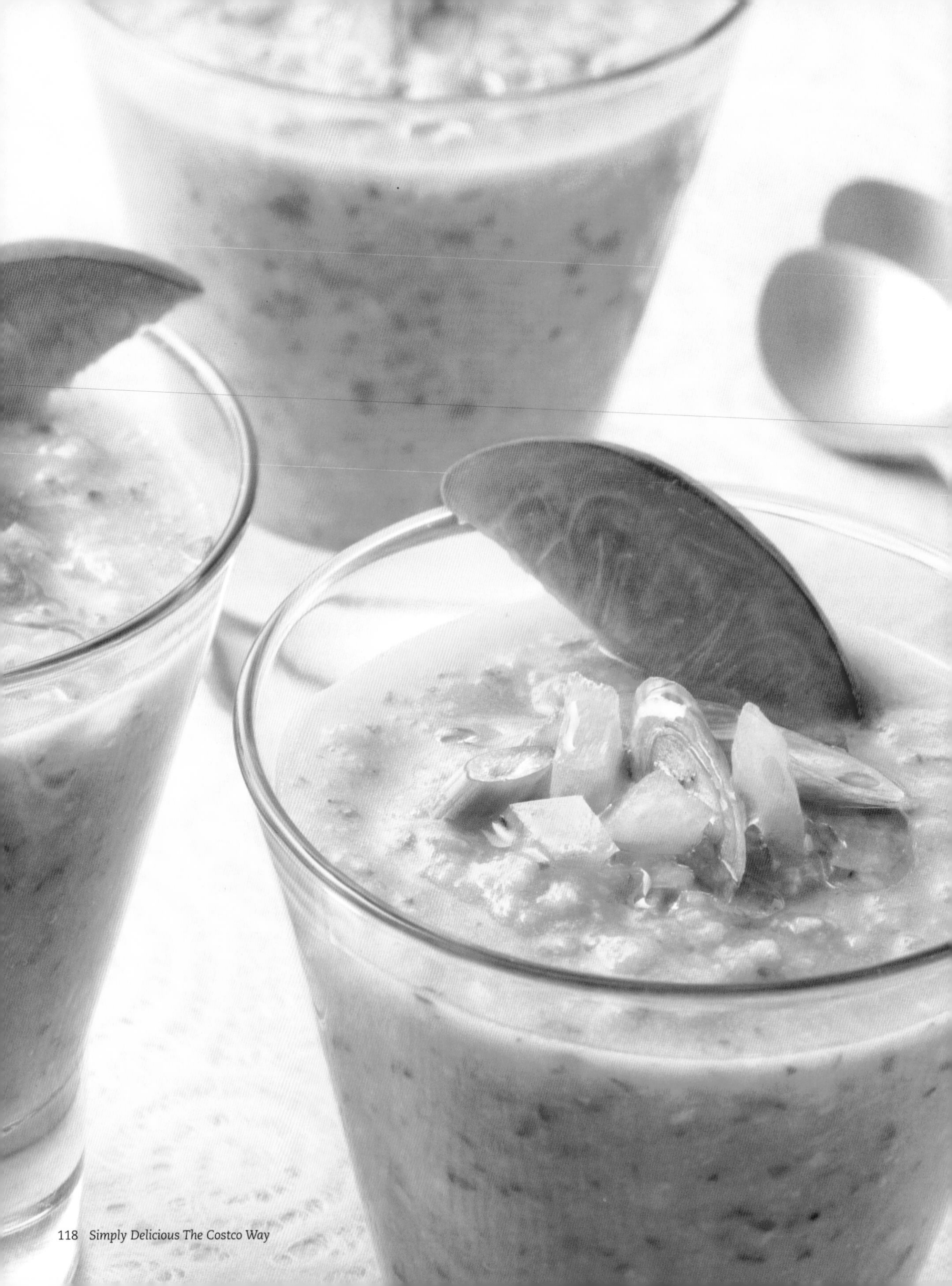

Mark Bittman

Mark Bittman is one of America's most widely respected food writers. He covers food policy, cooking and eating as an opinion columnist and blogger for The New York Times, *where he is also the* Sunday *Magazine's lead food writer. He has authored more than a dozen cookbooks, including* How to Cook Everything *and* Food Matters. *Learn more at howtocookeverything.com and markbittman.com.*

ROMULO YANES

Fresh Peach Gazpacho
Trinity Fruit

Recipes developed by Mark Bittman

2½ pounds fresh Trinity peaches, halved and pitted (peeled if you like)

1 medium cucumber, peeled, seeded and cut into chunks

2-3 thick bread slices (a day or two old is best), crusts removed, torn into small pieces

¼ cup olive oil, plus more for garnish

2 tablespoons any wine vinegar, or more to taste

1 medium garlic clove, cut in half

Salt and freshly ground black pepper

½ red or yellow bell pepper, cored, seeded and chopped, for garnish

2 scallions, chopped, for garnish

Cut peaches into quarters and put them in a blender or food processor with cucumber, bread, oil, vinegar, garlic and 1 cup water. Sprinkle with salt and pepper and pulse the machine on and off until smooth. If the mixture seems too thick, thin it by gradually adding water, 1 tablespoon at a time.

Taste and adjust the seasoning with salt, pepper and/or vinegar.

Serve right away, or refrigerate and eat within a couple of hours. Garnish each serving with bell pepper, scallions and a drizzle of olive oil. Makes 4 servings.

Fresh Plum Salsa
Trinity Fruit

1½ pounds Trinity fresh plums

1 medium white onion or 4 scallions, chopped

1-2 fresh hot green chiles (like jalapeño), seeded and minced

2 teaspoons minced garlic

1 cup chopped fresh basil or mint leaves (about 1 large bunch)

3 tablespoons fresh lime juice, or more to taste

Salt and freshly ground black pepper

Cut each plum in half lengthwise and remove the pits; don't bother to peel. Cut each half into wedges, then chop into small chunks. Scrape the pieces and all the juice on the cutting board into a large bowl.

Add onion, chile, garlic, basil and lime juice to the plums. Sprinkle with salt and pepper, then taste and adjust the seasoning, adding more lime juice if you like.

If you have time, let the salsa sit at room temperature for 15 minutes for the flavors to blend. (You can make the salsa ahead and refrigerate it for up to 2 hours; bring it back to room temperature before serving.)

Serve with chips. Makes 6-8 servings.

ABBY GREENAWALT

Meaghan Mountford

Meaghan Mountford stumbled into a cooking-decorating career almost 15 years ago. She will turn any dessert into edible art; she is especially fond of decorated cookies, painted marshmallows and sweets on sticks. Her latest book is Sugarlicious: 50 Cute and Clever Treats for Every Occasion *(Harlequin, 2012). Her blog is* The Decorated Cookie *(www.thedecoratedcookie.com), and she's the Edible Crafts editor for CraftGossip.com.*

Sheet Cake Cookie Crisps
CSM Bakery Products

Recipes developed by Meaghan Mountford

These melt-in-your-mouth cookies are a perfect combination of crispy and chewy, and they are quick and easy to make with your leftover Costco sheet cake. The more colorful the icing decorations, the more colorful your cookies will be. And the beauty of these cookies is that you can make them from any amount of cake, even just one slice.

¼ of a Kirkland Signature decorated white half-sheet cake, chilled

Preheat oven to 375°F. Line a baking sheet with parchment paper.

Place cake, with icing, in a large bowl. If you are using a quarter of the cake, work in 2 batches, or ⅛ of the cake at a time. Mix the cake and icing with a fork until it is just blended and a wet mixture forms. (If using a custard-filled cake, remove the filling before mixing.)

Use a ½-ounce ice cream scoop to form balls of dough about 1 inch in diameter. Place the balls of dough 2 inches apart on the prepared pan. Gently flatten the tops of the cookies with your hand.

Bake for 18-20 minutes, or until the entire top surfaces of the cookies are golden brown. These are best served warm. They keep in a sealed container for up to a week. Makes 56 cookies.

Tip: Save icing flowers to use as decorations on the cookie crisps.

Muffin Fries with Yogurt-Honey Dip
CSM Bakery Products

Bring a bit of the appetizer sensibility to the breakfast table with muffin "fries" and dip. Keep these on hand for nighttime snacking or a quick bite in the morning, or serve as an unusual finger food at a brunch. You can use any of the Kirkland Signature muffins, though the blueberry muffin fries are my favorites. For a sweeter treat, sprinkle the sticks with granulated sugar instead of sea salt.

4 Kirkland Signature muffins, any flavor
3 tablespoons butter
Sea salt

YOGURT-HONEY DIP
1 6-ounce container (¾ cup) plain Greek-style yogurt
2 tablespoons honey
2 tablespoons peanut butter (optional)

Preheat oven to 400°F. Line a baking sheet with parchment paper.

With a serrated knife, cut muffins into ½-inch-thick slices, then cut each muffin slice in half lengthwise. Arrange the muffin slices on the prepared baking sheet.

In a small saucepan on the stovetop or in a microwave-safe bowl in the microwave, melt the butter on a low setting. With a pastry brush, brush the tops of the muffin slices with the melted butter. Lightly sprinkle with sea salt.

Bake for 12-15 minutes, or until golden brown.

Prepare the dip: In a bowl, whisk together yogurt and honey. If desired, whisk in peanut butter. Store, covered, in the refrigerator for up to a week.

The muffin fries are best served warm, with the dip. Makes about 40 fries.

Entrées

Seared Scallops with Arugula Salad, Clementines and Pomegranate Gastrique
Atlantic Capes Fisheries

2 tablespoons olive oil

1½ pounds Atlantic Capes sea scallops (24), thawed in the refrigerator

Salt and pepper

1 clementine (or tangerine), peeled and sectioned

4 ounces Parmigiano-Reggiano cheese, shaved

POMEGRANATE GASTRIQUE

2 cups sugar

1 cup rice wine vinegar

1 cup pomegranate juice

ARUGULA SALAD

2 tablespoons extra-virgin olive oil

Juice of 1 lime

1 garlic clove, minced

½ teaspoon brown mustard

½ teaspoon honey

Salt and pepper

2 cups arugula, cleaned

Prepare the gastrique: Combine sugar, vinegar and pomegranate juice in a saucepan. Bring to a boil, then reduce the heat and simmer until the liquid is a syrup (15-20 minutes). Set aside.

Prepare the salad: Whisk together oil, lime juice, garlic, mustard, honey, and salt and pepper to taste. Toss the arugula with the dressing and place a mound of it on each plate.

Heat oil in a sauté pan over high heat. Season scallops with salt and pepper. Add the scallops to the very hot pan and sear on each side until golden brown (about 2 minutes per side).

Arrange the scallops around the arugula. Top the arugula with clementines. Drizzle each plate with the gastrique and top with the shaved cheese. Makes 4 servings.

Grilled Bacon-Wrapped Shrimp and Scallops with Peaches
American Pride Seafoods

8 American Pride Seafoods sea scallops, thawed

8 U15 shrimp, thawed

16 slices bacon

4 wooden skewers, soaked in water for 1 hour

4 peaches, quartered

4 green onions, thinly sliced

HOISIN BARBECUE SAUCE

1 cup hoisin sauce

¼ cup chili sauce

2 tablespoons honey

3 tablespoons soy sauce

2 tablespoons rice wine vinegar

1½ teaspoons sesame oil

1 tablespoon minced peeled ginger

4 garlic cloves, minced

2 tablespoons minced shallot

Preheat the grill to low and brush the grate with oil.

Wrap scallops and shrimp in bacon. Thread 2 shrimp and 2 scallops onto each skewer, alternating.

Prepare the sauce: Combine all ingredients and whisk together.

Grill the skewers for 6 minutes on each side, or to an internal temperature of 145°F, occasionally brushing with the sauce.

Grill peaches for 2-3 minutes on each side. After grilling, toss lightly with sauce.

Serve the scallop and shrimp skewers over the peaches and garnish with green onions. Makes 4 servings.

Curried Shrimp with Pineapple
Del Monte Fresh Produce

1 tablespoon canola oil

½ cup thinly sliced fresh Del Monte onion

1½ pounds large shrimp, shelled and deveined

2 tablespoons curry powder

1 fresh Del Monte green bell pepper, seeded and cut into thin strips

2 cups fresh Del Monte Gold Extra Sweet pineapple, chopped

1 fresh Del Monte mango, cut into thin strips

1¼ cups light coconut milk

2 tablespoons fish sauce

1 teaspoon Sriracha (Thai hot sauce), or to taste

1 teaspoon sugar

⅓ cup chopped fresh basil

Cooked jasmine rice, for serving

Heat oil in a large skillet over medium heat. Add onion and cook until soft. Push to the side of the skillet.

Add shrimp and curry powder; cook for about 2 minutes on each side.

Add bell pepper and stir the ingredients in the skillet together. Cook until the pepper softens.

Add pineapple, mango, coconut milk, fish sauce, Sriracha and sugar. Simmer for about 2-4 minutes. Remove from the heat and sprinkle with basil.

Serve over jasmine rice. Makes 4 servings.

Island Kabobs with Tropical Fruit Salsa

Dole

2 ripe, firm Dole bananas, peeled, each cut into 6 pieces, plus 1 ripe Dole banana, peeled and diced

12 chunks Dole Tropical Gold fresh pineapple

16 extra-large or jumbo shrimp, shelled and deveined

1 green or red bell pepper, cut into 8 pieces

4 Dole white or brown mushrooms, cut in half

2 tablespoons lime juice

2 tablespoons olive oil

½ teaspoon ground allspice

1 mango, peeled and diced

1 tablespoon chopped fresh cilantro or mint

1 Dole green onion, minced

2-3 teaspoons minced jalapeño

Preheat the grill to medium-high.

Thread 12 banana pieces, pineapple, shrimp, bell pepper and mushrooms onto skewers.

In a small bowl, whisk together lime juice, oil and allspice. Brush 2 tablespoons of the mixture over the kabobs.

Combine the remaining marinade with the diced banana, mango, cilantro or mint, green onion and jalapeño. Place in a serving dish.

Grill the kabobs for 8-10 minutes, turning once, or until the shrimp are opaque. Arrange the kabobs on top of the salsa. Makes 4 servings.

Nutritional information: Each serving has 217 calories, 6 g protein, 34 g carbohydrates, 8 g fat, 43 mg cholesterol, 5 g fiber, 52 mg sodium, 18 g sugar.

Crab en Papillote with Baked Scalloped Potatoes

Reser's Fine Foods

Quick & Easy

40-ounce tray Main Street Bistro Baked Scalloped Potatoes

Parchment paper

1 pound fresh crabmeat

½ cup chopped fresh chives

2 tablespoons melted butter

Preheat oven to 350°F.

Divide the scalloped potatoes into 12 equal squares.

For each serving, cut out a 12-by-16-inch piece of parchment paper and fold it in half. Draw a large half heart on the parchment, with the fold being the center of the heart. Cut out the heart shape and open.

Lay a spoonful of crab on the parchment in the center to one side of the fold. Lay a square of scalloped potatoes on top, followed by another spoonful of crab. Sprinkle with chives. Fold the other side of the heart over, and starting at the top, fold up both edges of parchment, overlapping the folds as you move along. Once you reach the end tip, twist several times and secure tightly. Place on a baking sheet and brush with melted butter.

Bake for 7 minutes. Open the parchment and serve. Makes 12 servings.

Dungeness Crab and Sweet Onion au Gratin
Pacific Seafood Group

This simple yet elegant recipe is a must-serve for special or festive events. I've been told by several event hosts, and I quote, "Should something arise that would prevent my attendance, please call and we will send a car to pick up the au gratin." This makes a perfect entrée, appetizer or side dish. Try it, and you'll call and thank me.

¼ pound Swiss cheese, shredded

½ teaspoon ground nutmeg

1 tablespoon grated lemon zest

½ cup flour

2 tablespoons salted butter

3 large sweet onions, thinly sliced

1 pound Dungeness crab meat

¾ cup Kirkland Signature mayonnaise

Juice of 1 small lemon

½ cup chopped fresh parsley

1 tablespoon sugar

Salt

White pepper

A few dashes of Tabasco sauce for a nice little kick (your choice)

Preheat oven to 375°F.

In a bowl, combine and toss cheese, nutmeg, lemon zest and flour. Set aside.

In a large sauté pan over medium heat, melt butter and sauté onions until translucent and tender. Set aside to cool.

In a large mixing bowl, combine crab, the cheese mixture, the onions, mayonnaise, lemon juice, parsley, sugar, salt and pepper to taste, and Tabasco. Mix very gently. Transfer to a large baking dish.

Bake in the center of the oven for 35-45 minutes, or until it bubbles slightly and is lightly browned. Makes 6 servings (12-14 as an appetizer).

Recipe developed by Gary R. Puetz.

JOHN KEATING

DAN OBRADOVICH
Manager, Pacific Seafood

Dungeness crab is a treasure from the ocean. Pacific Seafood harvests only male crabs at the peak of their quality and physical condition so Costco members can enjoy legs and claws that are succulent and full of meat.

The best thing about Dungeness crab is the flavor. A close second is the joyful experience you get from cracking and eating it. For the timid or uninitiated, digging into a crab couldn't be easier. First, twist off each leg where it joins the body. Next, break off the big claws. Legs and claws can be broken with either a nutcracker or a small hammer. If you have trouble getting to the meat, a pick or cocktail fork works beautifully.

While it's hard to imagine having any leftovers, extra crab can be used in crab cakes, omelets, salads and sandwiches.

Dungeness crab has the power to turn an average evening into an unforgettable event. Pick up a few crabs, some bread and wine on your next visit to Costco, invite a couple of friends for dinner and let the "cracking" event begin.

Spicy Asian Beer-Steamed Crab
International Seafood Ventures

3 pounds cooked King Crab legs and/or Dungeness clusters (cleaned halves of whole crab)

3 12-ounce bottles good lager beer

2 lemongrass stalks, cut in half lengthwise

4-inch piece of fresh ginger, thinly sliced

3-4 Thai chilies, thinly sliced, divided

8 garlic cloves, peeled

4 limes, cut into wedges, divided

2 green onions, thinly sliced

½ bunch cilantro, finely chopped

4 tablespoons Vietnamese fish sauce

Rinse crab under cool running water to remove any external ice.

In a 6-quart pot with a steamer insert, combine beer, lemongrass, ginger, half of the chilies, garlic and half of the lime wedges. Bring the mixture to an aromatic boil. Place the crab gently in the steamer, and steam until it is warmed through, about 4-5 minutes. Remove and place the crab on a large serving platter.

Sprinkle the crab with the remaining chilies, green onions, cilantro and fish sauce. Fish sauce can also be served on the side for dipping. Place the remaining lime wedges on the platter around the crab. Makes 2-4 servings.

Planked Alaska Salmon with Asian Glaze
Icicle Seafoods

1 bunch green onions, trimmed and sliced lengthwise

2 pounds fresh Alaska salmon fillets or portions

3 tablespoons pure maple syrup

2 teaspoons grated fresh ginger

2 teaspoons fresh lime juice

2 teaspoons soy sauce

1½ teaspoons freshly minced garlic

Special equipment: wood plank (see note)

Soak wood plank in water for 30 minutes to 2 hours. Dry the plank with paper towels and spray-coat or lightly oil one side.

Place green onions on the oiled side of the plank. Top with salmon.

In a small bowl, blend remaining ingredients. Rub ½ to 1 teaspoon of the mixture on each salmon portion. Let stand for 5 minutes before cooking.

Heat the grill to medium-high.

Place the planked salmon on the grill using indirect heat (not directly over heat). Reduce the heat to medium, cover the grill and cook for 10-15 minutes, or just until the salmon is opaque throughout. Makes 4-6 servings.

Note: This recipe works great whether you use a plank or cook it straight on the grill.

Healthy Salmon
True Nature Seafood

½ cup olive oil

¼ cup balsamic vinegar

2 6-ounce True Nature Seafood
   salmon fillets, skin removed

4 garlic cloves, pressed

1 tablespoon chopped fresh cilantro

1 tablespoon chopped fresh basil

1½ teaspoons garlic salt

In a small bowl, mix together oil and vinegar.

Arrange salmon fillets in a shallow baking dish. Rub garlic onto the fillets, then pour the oil and vinegar over them, turning once to coat. Season with cilantro, basil and garlic salt. Set aside to marinate for 10 minutes.

Preheat the oven broiler.

Place the salmon about 6 inches from the heat source and broil for 15 minutes, turning once, or until browned on both sides and easily flaked with a fork. Brush occasionally with the sauce from the pan. Makes 2 servings.

Chantal's Miso Marinated Salmon

Marine Harvest

4 Marine Harvest fresh farmed Atlantic
  salmon portions (6-8 ounces each)
1 tablespoon olive oil
1 teaspoon sesame oil
1 large garlic clove, minced
4 ounces shiitake mushrooms,
  stemmed, caps sliced
1 large bok choy, cut crosswise
  into 1-inch-wide strips
Salt and pepper
Cooked basmati or jasmine rice,
  for serving

MARINADE

2 large garlic cloves, minced
⅓ cup chopped green onions
¼ cup low-sodium soy sauce
1 tablespoon mirin (Japanese
  rice wine) or dry sherry
2 teaspoons light brown sugar
1 teaspoon toasted sesame oil
2 tablespoons white miso paste
1 tablespoon sliced peeled ginger

Prepare the marinade: Using a food processor or blender, combine all ingredients.

In a glass baking dish, arrange salmon and coat with the marinade. Marinate in the refrigerator for 15-60 minutes. Preheat oven to 500°F.

Remove the salmon from the marinade and place on a baking sheet. Bake for about 8 minutes, or until just opaque in the center.

In a large nonstick pan, heat olive oil and sesame oil over high heat. Add garlic and mushrooms; sauté, stirring constantly, until the mushrooms are tender, 3-5 minutes. Add bok choy and cook for an additional 3 minutes, or until the leaves are wilted but still green and the stalks are still white. Season to taste with salt and pepper. Serve the salmon with rice and the mushroom and bok choy mixture. Makes 4 servings.

Citrus Roasted Salmon
Alaska Glacier Seafoods

2 teaspoons grated lemon zest

1 teaspoon grated orange zest

3 tablespoons lemon juice

3 tablespoons honey

2 tablespoons chili powder

2 teaspoons ground cumin

1 teaspoon salt

1 teaspoon coriander seeds, ground

½ teaspoon cayenne pepper

1 6-ounce can orange juice concentrate, thawed

4 6-ounce Alaska Glacier Seafoods fresh wild Alaska salmon fillets

1 orange, peeled and thinly sliced, for garnish

Fresh parsley, for garnish

Preheat oven to 400°F.

In a mixing bowl, combine lemon and orange zest, lemon juice, honey, chili powder, cumin, salt, coriander, cayenne and orange juice concentrate. Blend with a whisk.

Place salmon fillets on a broiler pan. Using a pastry brush, coat the fillets with some of the citrus sauce.

Place the remaining sauce in a saucepan and cook over medium-high heat until reduced to about ½ cup.

Roast the salmon for 15 minutes, or until tender or almost opaque throughout.

Transfer the salmon to plates and top with the reduced sauce. Garnish with orange slices and parsley. Serve immediately. Makes 4 servings.

"In a Heartbeat" Ginger-Honey Salmon
Camanchaca

3 ounces sake

2 tablespoons soy sauce

1 tablespoon finely chopped fresh ginger

Cracked pepper to taste

4 6-ounce portions fresh skinless, boneless Camanchaca salmon

Honey to taste

Lemon or lime wedges (optional)

Preheat the oven broiler.

In a bowl, mix sake, soy sauce, ginger and cracked pepper. Pour into a shallow casserole dish.

Pierce salmon portions with a fork and place in the casserole. Baste with the marinade and drizzle generously with honey.

Place the casserole under the broiler on the top oven rack. Watch closely until salmon begins to brown, approximately 3-5 minutes.

Remove from the oven and turn the salmon. Baste with marinade and generously drizzle with honey. Continue broiling for 3-5 minutes, or until browned.

Serve with lemon or lime wedges for squeezing over the salmon. Makes 4 servings.

Steelhead with Strawberry Glaze

AquaGold Seafood

1 2-pound steelhead fillet

Salt and pepper

1 cup chopped
  fresh strawberries

½ cup good
  balsamic vinegar

½ cup water

½ cup organic blue
  agave nectar

1 cup sliced fresh
  strawberries, for serving

Preheat oven to 425°F.

Place steelhead, skin side down, on a lightly oiled baking sheet. Season to taste with salt and pepper.

While the oven is warming, combine chopped strawberries, vinegar and water in a saucepan. Cook over medium to medium-low heat until reduced by half. Puree the mixture. Return to the saucepan, add agave nectar and cook until reduced by a quarter. Remove from the heat.

Place the steelhead in the oven and bake for about 10 minutes, or until the fish lifts easily away from the skin.

To serve, remove the skin and dark meat from the steelhead. Spoon the sauce over the fish and top with sliced strawberries. Makes 4-6 servings.

Grilled Salmon with Savory Blueberry Citrus Sauce

AJ Trucco/Blossom Hill/Fillmore-Piru Citrus/Nature's Partner/Mulholland Citrus/The Oppenheimer Group

¾ cup vegetable stock

¼ cup balsamic vinegar

¼ cup fresh-squeezed
  clementine, navel
  orange or Murcott
  mandarin juice

2 tablespoons fresh-
  squeezed lemon juice

1 teaspoon honey

1 cup fresh blueberries

¼ cup chopped fresh chives

4 6-ounce salmon steaks

2 tablespoons olive oil

Sea salt

Freshly ground pepper

In a saucepan, mix vegetable stock, vinegar, citrus juices and honey. Bring to a boil over high heat, then reduce the heat to medium. Stir and cook until the sauce thickens and turns clear, about 1-2 minutes. Add blueberries and chives. Keep warm over low heat.

Meanwhile, preheat the grill to medium-high.

Brush salmon on both sides with oil and season to taste with salt and pepper. Grill until the salmon flakes easily with a fork, about 4 minutes per side.

Serve immediately with the blueberry citrus sauce. Makes 4 servings.

Asian Delight
True Nature Seafood

2 tablespoons low-sodium soy sauce
1 tablespoon miso (soybean paste)
1 tablespoon honey

4 6-ounce True Nature Seafood
salmon fillets, skin removed
Garlic powder
1 tablespoon chopped fresh chives,
or green onion curls

In a small bowl, whisk together soy sauce, miso and honey.

Place salmon in a dish, pour the marinade over and turn to coat. Cover and marinate for 30 minutes in the refrigerator. Preheat oven to 350°F.

Transfer the salmon from the marinade to a pan. Season with a sprinkle of garlic powder. Bake for 15 minutes, or until the fish flakes easily with a fork. Switch the oven to broil, and broil until the tops are browned and bubbly, about 3 minutes. Sprinkle with chives or green onions. Makes 4 servings.

Easy Salmon with Dill Dijon Sauce

Multiexport Foods

4 6- to 7-ounce Multiexport farmed
   salmon fillets (skinless)

Kosher salt and freshly ground
   black pepper

1½ tablespoons olive oil

3½ tablespoons unsalted butter, divided

1 small shallot, finely chopped

½ cup dry white wine

1½ tablespoons Dijon mustard

2 tablespoons chopped fresh dill,
   plus more for garnish

1 cucumber, thinly sliced

Preheat the broiler to high. Place salmon in a broiler pan. Season to taste with salt and pepper. Broil on the upper-middle oven rack until it is opaque in color and flakes easily, about 8-10 minutes.

In a saucepan, combine oil and 1 tablespoon butter. Heat over medium-high heat until the butter melts. Add shallot and cook until soft, about 1-2 minutes. Add wine and cook until reduced by half, about 3 minutes, whisking occasionally.

Reduce the heat to low and whisk in mustard, dill, ¼ teaspoon salt and ⅛ teaspoon pepper. Remove from the heat and add the remaining butter to the sauce in small pieces, whisking until blended.

Place the salmon on individual plates, spoon the sauce over the top and sprinkle with dill. Serve with the cucumber slices. Makes 4 servings.

Variation: Add some fresh lemon juice to the salmon prior to broiling.

Multiexport Foods
Nourishing the future

Captain Jack's Gingered Salmon
Multiexport Foods

⅓ cup sugar

¼ cup apple cider vinegar

½ cup soy sauce

½ teaspoon sesame oil

2 garlic cloves, peeled and minced

2 teaspoons ground ginger

8-10 slices pickled ginger

¾ cup ginger beer or ginger ale

4 6-ounce fresh Multiexport farmed salmon fillets (skinless)

In a bowl, combine sugar, vinegar and soy sauce, stirring until the sugar is dissolved. Add sesame oil, garlic, ground ginger, pickled ginger and ginger beer. Mix well.

Set aside a small amount of marinade to brush on the salmon while cooking. Marinate the salmon in the remaining marinade in the refrigerator for 4 hours.

To bake: Preheat oven to 400°F. Place marinated salmon portions in a baking dish on the middle oven rack and bake for 15 minutes, brushing with the reserved marinade. The salmon is done when it is opaque and flakes easily with a fork (internal temperature of 145°F).

To grill: Preheat the grill to medium-high. Place marinated salmon portions on a piece of aluminum foil on the grill and cook for approximately 15-20 minutes over medium heat, brushing with the reserved marinade. Makes 4 servings.

Multiexport Foods
Nourishing the future

Grilled Wild Alaska Sockeye Salmon
Copper River Seafoods

6 tablespoons low-sodium soy sauce

4 tablespoons olive oil, plus more for brushing

2 tablespoons Worcestershire sauce

1 teaspoon grated lemon zest

1 teaspoon fresh lemon juice

1 teaspoon chopped fresh parsley

4 6-ounce portions Kirkland Signature fresh wild Alaska sockeye salmon

Kosher salt and white pepper

Preheat the grill on high until very hot.

To prepare the basting sauce, combine soy sauce, oil, Worcestershire sauce, lemon zest, lemon juice and parsley. Set aside for 10 minutes to allow the flavors to blend.

Lightly brush salmon with oil and season to taste with salt and pepper.

Place the salmon on the grill and cook for 2 minutes. Turn the salmon over and cook for another 2 minutes. Turn again, this time rotating at a 90-degree angle, to achieve a hatch pattern. After 2 minutes, turn once more at 90 degrees and cook for a final 2 minutes, or until it flakes easily with a fork.

Just before removing the salmon from the grill, brush each portion generously with the baste. Serve immediately. Makes 4 servings.

Recipe courtesy of Bridge Seafood Restaurant in Anchorage, Alaska.

Wild Alaska Smoked Salmon and Cherry Tomato Wraps
Copper River Seafoods

3 15-ounce cans white beans

5 ounces white bean juice, reserved from cans

1 teaspoon grated lemon zest

¼ cup fresh lemon juice (2 lemons)

3 tablespoons chopped fresh parsley, plus more for garnish

3 teaspoons Kirkland Signature Sweet Mesquite Seasoning

Salt and pepper

24 ounces Copper River Seafoods smoked sockeye salmon

8 large flour tortillas

1 romaine heart

16 fresh red cherry tomatoes, cut in half lengthwise

Drain beans, reserving 5 ounces of the liquid. Rinse the beans.

In a bowl, combine the beans, bean juice, lemon zest and lemon juice. Mash together with a stiff whisk or fork. A few beans should be left whole and broken for texture. Add parsley, mesquite seasoning, and salt and pepper to taste, then mix again.

Remove skin from the salmon and flake into large chunks. Carefully fold into the bean mixture.

Fill each tortilla with romaine leaves, smoked salmon/bean mixture and tomato halves. Roll up tightly to enclose the filling. Cut each wrap in half and garnish with parsley. Makes 8 servings.

ALASKA FX PRODUCTIONS

ROB KINNEEN
Chef

Alaska sockeye salmon are world-renowned for their rich flavor and distinctive deep red color. Preserve the quality of your Copper River Seafoods salmon by following a few simple tips.

- *When cooking salmon—fresh or thawed—be sure to remove your fish from the refrigerator 7-10 minutes before cooking to "temp" it.*

- *Refrain from adding salt until just before cooking in the pan or on the grill. Salt will pull moisture to the surface of the salmon if it's left to sit.*

- *Before seasoning, use a paper towel to remove excess moisture from the salmon, which will result in a nicely seared surface with minimal sticking to the pan.*

- *To prevent the salmon from becoming dry, remove the fish from the heat as soon as it flakes easily with a fork or is opaque throughout.*

- *For best flavor and texture, salmon should not be refrozen and should be eaten within two days.*

Spinach and Feta Stuffed Salmon
BluMar

8 ounces cream cheese

1 cup mayonnaise

1 10-ounce package frozen chopped spinach, thawed and drained

¼ cup crumbled feta cheese

2 tablespoons grated Parmesan cheese

2 garlic cloves, chopped

¼ cup chopped onion

1 teaspoon ground nutmeg

1 teaspoon crushed red pepper flakes

1 tablespoon lemon juice

1 cup panko bread crumbs

2¼ pounds fresh salmon, cut into 6 fillets

Preheat oven to 375°F.

In a medium bowl, mix cream cheese, mayonnaise, spinach, feta, Parmesan and garlic until well blended. Fold in onion, nutmeg, red pepper flakes, lemon juice and bread crumbs. Set aside.

Carefully cut a 3-inch horizontal slit along the side of each salmon fillet, moving the knife back and forth to form a pocket. Spoon the spinach mixture into the pockets. Place on a baking pan.

Bake for 12-16 minutes, or until the stuffing is golden brown or a thermometer inserted in the center registers 165°F. Makes 4-6 servings.

Steve's Smoked Salmon Lasagna
Marine Harvest

1 16-ounce package Royal Fjord Hot Smoked Roasted Salmon

16 ounces ricotta cheese

¼ cup chopped fresh basil

¼ cup chopped fresh parsley

½ cup Riesling wine (optional)

16 ounces lasagna noodles

4 cups Kirkland Signature marinara sauce

Salt and pepper

24 ounces shredded Italian cheese blend

2 cups fresh spinach

Preheat oven to 375°F.

In a bowl, break up smoked salmon into small pieces. Add ricotta, basil, parsley and wine; mix well.

Cook lasagna noodles according to package directions.

In a deep 13-by-9-inch baking dish, pour a thin layer of marinara sauce. Layer some of the lasagna noodles in the dish, slightly overlapping. Lightly season the noodles with salt and pepper. Pour on another thin layer of marinara sauce. Add a third of the smoked salmon mixture, a third of the shredded cheese and a layer of spinach leaves. Pour another thin layer of marinara sauce over the spinach.

Repeat the layers twice. Finish with a top layer of noodles, covered with sauce and shredded cheese.

Cover and bake for 30 minutes. Remove the cover and bake for another 30 minutes. Let rest for 10 minutes before slicing. Makes 8-10 servings.

Brown Sugar Citrus Tilapia

Sunkist Growers

1 tablespoon finely grated fresh Sunkist lemon zest

1 tablespoon finely grated fresh Sunkist orange zest

⅓ cup flour

½ teaspoon freshly ground black pepper

½ teaspoon chili powder

1½ pounds tilapia fillets (4 fillets)

3 tablespoons butter, divided

1 garlic clove, minced

1 tablespoon fresh Sunkist lemon juice

1 tablespoon fresh Sunkist orange juice

1 Sunkist lemon, thinly sliced

1 Sunkist orange, thinly sliced

1½ tablespoons light brown sugar

4 fresh parsley sprigs, for garnish

In a shallow bowl, combine lemon zest, orange zest, flour, black pepper and chili powder; blend well. Pat dry tilapia fillets and place in the seasoning, coating both sides well.

Melt 2 tablespoons butter in a large frying pan over medium-high heat. Place tilapia in the pan and sauté for 5-6 minutes, turning once. Both sides should be a nice golden brown.

Remove the fillets from the pan and add 1 tablespoon butter, garlic, lemon juice and orange juice; cook for 30 seconds. Add lemon and orange slices, sprinkle with brown sugar and cook over medium heat for 2-3 minutes, or until they start to caramelize. Add tilapia to the pan and coat well with pan sauce.

To serve, place the tilapia on plates and cover with the caramelized lemon and orange slices. Garnish with parsley and serve immediately. Makes 4 servings.

Sunkist

Tilapia with Coconut Rice and Papaya Chutney
Slade Gorton

1½ cups basmati rice

4 portions Gourmet Bay Toasted
  Breadcrumb Tilapia

¼ cup roughly chopped fresh mint

¼ cup roughly chopped fresh cilantro

1 14-ounce can coconut milk

Salt and pepper

Preheat oven to 375°F.

Prepare the chutney: In a bowl, combine all ingredients and stir to blend.

SPICY PAPAYA CHUTNEY

½ cup peeled and diced papaya

½ cup peeled and diced pineapple

Grated zest and juice of 1 lime

½ cup Major Grey's chutney

2 tablespoons chopped green onion

2 teaspoons crushed red pepper flakes

Cook rice according to package directions, until tender and fluffy.

Meanwhile, place tilapia on a sheet pan and bake for 10-12 minutes, or until the internal temperature is 165°F.

Toss the cooked rice with mint, cilantro, coconut milk, and salt and pepper to taste. Keep warm.

To serve, place the fish on the rice and top with chutney. Makes 4 servings.

Baked Tilapia with Tomato Tartar Sauce
Rain Forest Aquaculture

1 medium leek, well washed and quartered

2 medium carrots, peeled and quartered lengthwise

2 medium celery stalks, halved lengthwise

4 Rain Forest Aquaculture tilapia fillets

2 tablespoons olive oil

Salt and pepper

1 medium lemon, cut into 8 thin slices

4 sprigs fresh rosemary

TARTAR SAUCE

½ cup mayonnaise

1 tablespoon chopped cornichons (gherkins)

1 teaspoon chopped shallot

1 teaspoon chopped fresh chives

1 teaspoon roasted tomato puree

Preheat oven to 350°F. Oil a 13-by-9-inch baking dish.

Arrange leek, carrots and celery in the prepared pan.

Rub tilapia fillets with oil and season to taste with salt and pepper. Place 2 slices of lemon and 1 sprig of rosemary on top of each piece.

Arrange the fish on the vegetables. Bake for 20 minutes, or until the flesh is opaque.

Prepare tartar sauce: In a small bowl, mix together mayonnaise, cornichons, shallot, chives and tomato puree. Season to taste with salt and pepper.

To serve, arrange the tilapia on a platter and surround with the vegetables and the tartar sauce. Makes 4 servings.

Tilapia with Red Pepper Sauce
Divine Flavor

1 Divine Flavor red bell pepper

1 teaspoon olive oil, plus more for grilling

¼ cup chopped green onions

¼ cup mayonnaise

2 teaspoons smoky chipotle sauce

4 Kirkland Signature frozen tilapia loins, thawed

Salt and pepper

1 tablespoon chopped Divine Flavor red bell pepper

1 tablespoon chopped Divine Flavor orange bell pepper

1 tablespoon chopped Divine Flavor yellow bell pepper

Preheat the grill to high.

Cut red bell pepper in quarters, remove seeds, and cut off the ends where the pepper curls. Coat pepper with oil. Place on the grill skin side down and grill for 20-25 minutes, or until charred. Let cool, then peel off the skin.

In a food processor, puree the grilled pepper, 1 teaspoon oil, green onions, mayonnaise and chipotle sauce.

Season tilapia with salt and pepper to taste. Grill over medium heat until it is opaque and the juices run clear, 3-4 minutes per side.

In a bowl, combine the chopped red, orange and yellow peppers.

Remove the fish from the heat and place on plates. Garnish with the sauce and chopped peppers. Makes 4 servings.

Grilled Tilapia with Lemon Crème Fraîche and Fresh Herbs

Kirkland Signature/Regal Springs

½ cup lightly packed watercress leaves and small sprigs, chopped (leave a few whole for garnish)

¼ cup chopped fresh dill sprigs

¼ cup chopped fresh tarragon leaves

Salt

Olive oil

6 Kirkland Signature/Regal Springs frozen tilapia loins, thawed (see note)

Roasted root vegetables or cooked rice, for serving

LEMON CRÈME FRAÎCHE

3 large lemons, halved

3 tablespoons olive oil

3 tablespoons crème fraîche (or sour cream)

2 teaspoons Dijon mustard

Sea salt and freshly ground black pepper

Prepare the lemon crème fraîche: Heat a griddle pan to high. Lightly oil the pan. Grill lemon halves cut side down for 5 minutes, or until soft and charred. Squeeze the lemon juice into a bowl. Add oil, crème fraîche and mustard; stir to blend. Season to taste with salt and pepper.

In a small mixing bowl, combine watercress, dill and tarragon. Season with a pinch of salt and a drizzle of olive oil. Set aside.

Heat a griddle pan to medium-high. Lightly oil the pan. Add tilapia and grill for 3-4 minutes per side, or until the flesh is opaque and flakes when cut with a fork.

Serve the tilapia with roasted root vegetables or rice. Top with lemon crème fraîche and the herb mixture. Makes 6 servings.

Note: To use frozen tilapia loins, place them on a baking pan lined with parchment paper and bake in a 375°F oven for 15 minutes.

RON BERG

DEBBIE GOLD
Chef

I'm impressed with this tilapia's clean taste and pure white color. It's versatile for so many protein recipes because of its neutral taste. These tilapia loins can stand in for any fish or chicken in a recipe, whether baked, sautéed or used in soups.

I also like this tilapia for its nutritional value: A 3.5-ounce serving of tilapia has only 98 calories and provides 18.5 grams of valuable protein—and no saturated fat.

Regal Springs is dedicated to setting the standard in sustainable fish farming. The company's entire process speaks of balance and health; not only do they carefully raise their tilapia in pristine remote water reservoirs, they also have built up the local infrastructures, including clinics and ambulances, and daycare for employees' children. When you buy this product, you take care of your health and the health of the communities from which these fish come.

Pan-Seared Tilapia with Zesty Grape Salsa
Kirschenman

1 teaspoon salt
1 teaspoon pepper
1 teaspoon paprika
½ teaspoon ground cumin
4 6-ounce tilapia fillets
2 tablespoons olive oil

ZESTY GRAPE SALSA
1 cup chopped grape tomatoes
1 cup diced Kirschenman green seedless grapes
1 cup diced Kirschenman red seedless grapes
½ cup chopped red onion
½ cup chopped red bell pepper

2 garlic cloves, diced
2 tablespoons diced jalapeño, vein and seeds removed
2 tablespoons chopped fresh mint
1 tablespoon olive oil
Juice of 1 lime
1 teaspoon salt

Meanwhile, combine salt, pepper, paprika and cumin. Season both sides of the tilapia with the mixture.

Heat oil in a sauté pan over medium heat until the oil begins to shimmer. Add the fish and cook for 5 minutes, then flip and cook on the other side for 5 more minutes, or until it is white and firm.

Serve with the salsa on top. Makes 4 servings.

Tip: The salsa can be made up to a day ahead and stored, covered, in the refrigerator.

Prepare the salsa: Place all ingredients in a bowl and mix well. Let stand for at least 30 minutes before serving for best flavor.

White Fish and Tomato Fricassee
Mastronardi Produce/SUNSET

2 6-ounce white fish fillets
Kirkland Signature sea salt
Freshly ground black pepper
2 tablespoons cooking oil, divided
12 ounces wild mushrooms
2 tablespoons butter
2 small shallots, sliced

1 garlic clove, finely chopped
2 pounds SUNSET Zima grape tomatoes, halved
Splash of dry white wine
4 ounces 35% cream (whipping cream)
Fresh parsley, chopped
Dash of lemon juice

Preheat oven to 350°F.

Remove any small bones from fish. Season to taste with salt and pepper. In an ovenproof frying pan, heat 1 tablespoon oil over medium-high heat. Place the fish, flesh side down, in the pan and transfer the pan to the oven for 5-6 minutes, or until just cooked through.

Brush mushrooms with a pastry brush to clean. Break the mushrooms down by hand or cut into bite-size pieces.

In a frying pan, heat 1 tablespoon oil and butter over medium-high heat. Toss in shallots, garlic, mushrooms and tomatoes. Lower the heat and gently sauté. Add wine and cook until reduced by half. Add cream and reduce the fricassee until it thickens. Season to taste with salt, pepper and parsley. Just before serving, stir in lemon juice.

Top the fish with the fricassee. Makes 2 servings.

Recipe developed by chef Jason Rosso.

Goodness Grown Naturally®

Herbed Parmesan Panko Baked Flounder
Orca Bay

½ cup panko bread crumbs

¼ cup shredded Parmesan cheese

2 teaspoons dried Italian herb blend

Salt and pepper

2 tablespoons butter

4 Orca Bay Seafoods frozen flounder fillets, thawed

Parsley or thyme sprigs, for garnish

Preheat oven to 375°F.

In a shallow pan, mix panko, Parmesan and herbs. Season to taste with salt and pepper.

Melt butter on a large plate (about 1 minute on high in most microwaves).

Pat flounder fillets dry. Dip both sides in melted butter, then coat both sides with the panko mixture, pressing down to help the crumbs adhere. Lay the coated fillets on a baking sheet.

Bake for 14-15 minutes, or until the coating is just starting to turn a light brown and the fish is flaky. Garnish with parsley or thyme sprigs and serve immediately. Makes 4 servings.

ORCA BAY SEAFOODS, INC.

Miso-Glazed Halibut with Rosemary Roasted Potatoes
S.M. Products (BC) Ltd.

¼ cup low-sodium white miso paste

1 teaspoon brown sugar

½ cup sake

4 6-ounce halibut fillets

¼ cup olive oil

Sea salt and freshly ground pepper

ROSEMARY ROASTED POTATOES

1½ pounds small new potatoes, halved

¼ cup olive oil

¼ cup freshly grated Parmesan cheese (optional)

3 garlic cloves, minced

1 tablespoon fresh or dried rosemary leaves

Sea salt and freshly ground pepper to taste

Preheat oven to 400°F.

Prepare the potatoes: In a large bowl, toss all the ingredients together until evenly combined. Place on a baking sheet and bake for 20 minutes. Remove from the oven and gently toss and turn the potatoes. Roast for another 20 minutes, or until golden brown and tender.

Meanwhile, blend miso paste, brown sugar and sake in a small bowl.

Coat halibut fillets with oil and season to taste with salt and pepper. Sear the halibut in a non-stick pan over medium-high to high heat, about 2 minutes per side. Transfer to a lightly oiled baking sheet and spread the miso mixture on top. Bake for 15 minutes, or until flaky and opaque in the center. Makes 4 servings.

S.M. Products

WOONIA

Beer-Battered Fish and Chips
North Coast Seafoods

2 quarts vegetable oil, for frying

1½ cups all-purpose flour, sifted, plus more for dusting

1 teaspoon kosher salt

½ teaspoon ground black pepper

1 12-ounce can or bottle of beer

2 pounds North Coast Seafoods skinless haddock, cut into 4-ounce pieces

French fries, coleslaw and tartar sauce, for serving

Heat oil in a fryer or pot to 350°F.

In a bowl, combine flour, salt, pepper and beer; mix until smooth.

Dust each piece of haddock in plain flour and shake off all excess flour.

Dip in the beer batter and slowly place 3 or 4 pieces in the hot oil. Cook until the fish is floating and golden brown, about 5-6 minutes.

Carefully remove the fish from the oil and place on paper towels to drain. Continue with the remaining haddock.

Serve with French fries, coleslaw and tartar sauce. Makes 4 servings.

Grilled Catfish with Mango Salsa
Consolidated Catfish Producers

4 fresh U.S. farm-raised
  catfish fillets

2 teaspoons olive oil

1 teaspoon garlic salt

½ teaspoon cracked
  black pepper

¼ teaspoon ground
  red pepper

MANGO SALSA

1 cup diced fresh mango

1 cup diced fresh papaya

1 tablespoon minced
  green onion

1 tablespoon minced
  red jalapeño

2 tablespoons fresh
  lime juice

1 tablespoon honey

Prepare the salsa: Combine all ingredients in a bowl. Mix well. Let stand at room temperature for 20 minutes.

Preheat the grill.

Rinse catfish fillets and pat dry. Brush each fillet with ½ teaspoon oil.

In a small bowl, combine garlic salt, black pepper and red pepper. Sprinkle an equal amount on the rounded side of each fillet.

Grill the fillets over high heat, rounded side down, for 3-4 minutes. Turn the fillets over and grill for 3-4 minutes, or until the fish flakes easily with a fork.

Serve with the salsa. Makes 4 servings.

Chili-Tamari Trout
Clear Springs

½ cup chili garlic sauce

½ cup firmly packed
  light brown sugar

2 teaspoons tamari
  soy sauce

4 8-ounce Butterfly Style
  Clear•Cuts boneless
  rainbow trout fillets

8 green onions,
  sliced diagonally into
  1-inch pieces

⅓ cup sliced almonds,
  toasted

In a medium bowl, combine chili garlic sauce, brown sugar and soy sauce.

Heat a grill pan until hot. Add trout, flesh side down, and grill for 3 minutes. Turn, then spread evenly with the chili garlic mixture. Cook for 2-3 minutes, or until the trout is opaque.

Remove the trout to serving plates. Top with green onions and almonds. Serve immediately. Makes 4 servings.

Blackened Fresh Ahi Tuna
Western United Fish Company

2 tablespoons olive oil

2 tablespoons butter

2 Western United fresh ahi tuna steaks (about 2 pounds)

SEASONING

1 tablespoon paprika

1 teaspoon garlic powder

1 teaspoon onion powder

2 teaspoons salt

2 teaspoons ground black pepper

¼ teaspoon cayenne pepper (or to taste)

½ teaspoon dried oregano leaves

½ teaspoon dried thyme leaves

Prepare the seasoning: In a small bowl, mix all the ingredients. Transfer to a shaker.

Heat oil and butter in a heavy skillet over high heat. Let the pan get very hot before cooking.

Sprinkle both sides of ahi steaks with the seasoning, coating thoroughly. Place in the hot pan and cook for 2-3 minutes on each side, until the seasoning gets a charred look.

Remove from the pan and let rest for a few minutes. Slice into ¼-inch strips.

Serve with a mixed green salad or stir-fried vegetables. Makes 4 servings.

Your Direct Source

Hawaiian Select Tuna en Papillote
Norpac Fisheries Export/Kirkland Signature

Kirkland Signature Parchment Paper

4 8-ounce tuna steaks

1 red onion, sliced

1 beefsteak tomato, cut into 4 slices

1 green bell pepper, seeded and cut into rings

2 teaspoons finely chopped fresh oregano

Salt and pepper to taste

1 small green or red chile, seeded and finely chopped

4 tablespoons white wine or lemon juice

Preheat oven to 400°F.

Tear off four 15-inch sheets of parchment paper. Fold the sheets in half, crease and unfold.

For each serving, place 1 tuna steak on a parchment sheet near the crease. Top with 2 onion slices, 1 tomato slice and 2 bell pepper rings. Sprinkle with oregano, salt, pepper and chile. Spoon 1 tablespoon wine or lemon juice over the tuna. Fold the parchment paper over to enclose. Starting at the top corner, make small overlapping folds around the packet. Twist the last fold for a tight seal. Place on a baking sheet.

Bake for about 10-12 minutes.

Place the packets on plates. Carefully cut an X in the top of each packet to let the steam escape. Serve immediately, in or out of the packet. Makes 4 servings.

Change-of-Pace Tuna Casserole
Chicken of the Sea

1 10.75-ounce can condensed cream of mushroom soup, plus ½ to 1 can of milk for desired consistency

½ cup light sour cream

½ pound tricolor rotini pasta, cooked according to package directions

1 10-ounce package frozen chopped broccoli or mixed stir-fry vegetables, thawed

2 tablespoons chopped pimiento

2 tablespoons butter or margarine

8 ounces fresh mushrooms, sliced

½ cup chopped onion

½ cup chopped celery

2 7-ounce cans Chicken of the Sea chunk light tuna in water, drained

½ cup unsalted sliced almonds, toasted

Preheat oven to 350°F. Lightly grease a 1½-quart baking dish.

In a bowl, blend soup with milk and sour cream until smooth. Stir in pasta, broccoli and pimiento; set aside.

Melt butter in a sauté pan over medium heat. Add mushrooms, onion and celery, and cook until tender, about 5 minutes. Mix the vegetables into the soup mixture. Fold in tuna.

Pour into the prepared baking dish. Top with almonds.

Bake, uncovered, for about 25 minutes, or until hot and bubbly. Makes 4-6 servings.

South of the Border Tuna Enchiladas
Chicken of the Sea

2 7-ounce cans Chicken of the Sea chunk light tuna in water, drained

1 cup shredded Mexican-style cheese blend

⅓ cup corn kernels

⅓ cup minced red onion

2 tablespoons minced fresh cilantro

1 15-ounce can mild green chile enchilada sauce, divided

8 6-inch soft taco-size flour tortillas

⅓ cup sour cream

Preheat oven to 425°F.

In a medium bowl, flake tuna. Mix in cheese, corn, onion, cilantro and ⅔ cup enchilada sauce.

Spread 2 tablespoons of enchilada sauce in the bottom of an 8-by-8-inch baking dish.

Fill each tortilla with about ⅓ cup of the tuna mixture. Roll up and place seam-side down in the baking dish.

In a small bowl, mix the remaining enchilada sauce with sour cream. Pour over the rolled tortillas. Bake, uncovered, for 30 minutes, or until golden brown. Let the enchiladas sit for 5 minutes before serving. Makes 8 enchiladas.

Baked Chicken with Onion and Garlic Breading

Kirkland Signature/Olde Thompson

1 pound boneless, skinless chicken breasts, pounded to ¾- to 1-inch thickness

2 cups buttermilk

Olive oil

1½ cups panko bread crumbs

3 tablespoons Kirkland Signature chopped dehydrated onion

⅛ teaspoon Kirkland Signature granulated garlic

1 teaspoon Kirkland Signature sea salt

½ teaspoon Kirkland Signature Malabar ground pepper

2 tablespoons chopped fresh parsley

1 lemon, cut into wedges

Place chicken breasts in a shallow dish and pour buttermilk over to cover. Refrigerate for 1-4 hours. Remove from the refrigerator 20 minutes before baking.

Preheat oven to 375°F. Prepare a baking sheet by brushing with a thin layer of oil.

In a shallow dish, combine panko, dehydrated onion, granulated garlic, salt and pepper.

Remove chicken from the buttermilk, allowing excess buttermilk to drip off, and dredge in the panko mixture. Firmly press the bread crumbs into the chicken on both sides to generously coat. Shake excess coating off and transfer to the prepared baking sheet.

Drizzle the top of each piece of chicken with oil. Bake for 10-12 minutes, or until the chicken is firm and just cooked through.

Move the oven rack to the upper third of the oven and increase the oven setting to 450°F. Cook the chicken for 3-5 minutes, or until it is nicely browned, watching carefully to avoid burning.

Remove from the oven and sprinkle the chicken with parsley. Serve with lemon wedges. Makes 3-4 servings.

Honey-Glazed Chicken with Clementines
Duda Farm Fresh Foods

½ cup Dandy clementine juice (freshly squeezed)

1 tablespoon white balsamic vinegar

1 teaspoon sea salt

Freshly ground pepper

2 tablespoons extra-virgin olive oil

4 skinless chicken breasts, with the ribs

3 cups thinly sliced red onions

3 whole Dandy clementines

4 tablespoons honey

Place first 5 ingredients in a 1-gallon resealable plastic bag and shake to combine. Add chicken, seal the bag and refrigerate for 1 hour to overnight.

Preheat oven to 400°F.

Spread onions in an even layer in a baking dish just large enough to hold the chicken in 1 layer. Arrange the marinated chicken on top of the onions, reserving the marinade.

Slice each clementine, unpeeled, into 4 horizontal slices. Arrange 3 clementine slices on top of each chicken breast. Pour the marinade over the chicken and fruit. Drizzle 1 tablespoon of honey over each clementine-topped chicken breast. Cover the pan tightly with foil.

Bake for 20 minutes. Uncover and bake 15 minutes longer, or until the internal temperature of the chicken is 165°F. Remove from the oven and let sit for 10 minutes. Makes 4 servings.

Spicy Chicken with Grilled Stone Fruit, Mango and Kiwifruit
AJ Trucco/Blossom Hill/Fillmore-Piru Citrus/ Nature's Partner/Mulholland Citrus/ The Oppenheimer Group

½ cup olive oil, divided

4 garlic cloves, grated

2 tablespoons Worcestershire sauce

2 tablespoons Dijon mustard

2 tablespoons paprika

4 boneless, skinless chicken breasts

2 apricots, pitted and quartered

2 peaches, pitted and quartered

1 mango, peeled, pitted and cubed

2 kiwifruit, peeled and sliced

Sea salt

Freshly ground pepper

½ cup balsamic vinegar

2 tablespoons light brown sugar

2 sprigs fresh rosemary, leaves stripped and chopped

Preheat a grill or grill pan to medium-high.

In a large bowl, combine ¼ cup oil, garlic, Worcestershire sauce, mustard and paprika. Add chicken, coat evenly and marinate for 15 minutes. Grill, turning once, until the juices run clear and the chicken is cooked through, about 5 minutes on each side.

Meanwhile, lightly drizzle apricots, peaches, mango and kiwifruit with the remaining ¼ cup oil and season to taste with salt and pepper. Place on a lightly greased pan, place on the grill and cook until the fruit darkens and caramelizes on the edges, 4-5 minutes.

To make the sauce, mix vinegar, brown sugar and rosemary in a small saucepan and bring to a boil. Lower the heat and simmer until reduced by half, 6-7 minutes.

Serve the chicken immediately with the fruit alongside and the sauce drizzled over both. Makes 4 servings.

Grilled Chicken with California Avocado Red, White and Blueberry Salsa
California Avocado Commission

½ sweet white onion, minced

1 teaspoon minced fresh ginger

1 serrano chile, stemmed, seeded and minced

1 tablespoon low-sodium soy sauce

1 tablespoon canola oil

4 boneless, skinless chicken thighs

SALSA

½ sweet white onion, minced

2 ripe red tomatoes, diced

2 serrano chiles, stemmed, seeded and minced

1 tablespoon minced fresh mint, cilantro or basil

1 large ripe fresh California Avocado, peeled, seeded and diced

½ cup fresh blueberries

¼ teaspoon sea salt

Prepare the salsa: Gently combine all ingredients. Let rest for at least 10 minutes before serving to let the flavors blend.

To make the marinade, combine onion, ginger, chile, soy sauce and oil in a bowl. Place chicken in a gallon-size zip-lock bag. Add the marinade to the bag, seal and knead the bag to coat the chicken. Let rest at room temperature for 30-60 minutes. Discard the marinade.

Over a medium-hot grill, grill the chicken for about 10 minutes per side, or until cooked through. Top with salsa and serve. Makes 4 servings.

Nutritional information: Each serving has 220 calories, 16 g protein, 14 g carbohydrates, 12 g fat, 65 mg cholesterol, 4 g fiber, 320 mg sodium, 5 g sugar.

Citrus Roasted Chicken with Stone Fruit
AJ Trucco/Blossom Hill/Fillmore-Piru Citrus/ Nature's Partner/Mulholland Citrus/ The Oppenheimer Group

2 tablespoons olive oil, plus more for greasing

1 teaspoon sea salt

Freshly ground pepper to taste

2 tablespoons fresh-squeezed lemon juice

2 tablespoons fresh-squeezed easy-peel clementine, navel orange or Murcott mandarin juice

6 chicken thighs, skin on

1 red onion, peeled and thinly sliced

2 apricots, pitted and quartered

2 peaches, pitted and quartered

GARNISH

Slices of easy-peel clementine, navel orange or Murcott mandarin and 1 cup halved seedless grapes

Preheat oven to 400°F. Grease a 13-by-9-inch roasting pan with olive oil.

Combine salt, pepper and citrus juices in a large bowl. Add chicken and soak for 10 minutes.

Heat 2 tablespoons olive oil in a large skillet over medium-high heat. Add the chicken and cook until the skin is well browned on one side, about 5 minutes.

Place the chicken browned side up in the roasting pan. Add onion, apricots and peaches to the pan. Roast until the chicken is cooked through, about 40 minutes.

Transfer the chicken, onion, apricots and peaches to a plate. Garnish with slices of citrus and halved grapes. Serve immediately. Makes 6 servings.

Tikka Masala Chicken
Kirkland Signature/Tyson

4 Kirkland Signature boneless, skinless chicken breasts

2 tablespoons butter, divided

1 teaspoon lime juice

1 tablespoon chopped fresh cilantro

CHICKEN TIKKA PASTE

1 tablespoon lemon juice

1 tablespoon red chili paste

2 teaspoons salt

1 teaspoon sugar

¼ teaspoon ground black pepper

YOGURT MASALA MARINADE

1 cup plain yogurt

1 teaspoon chopped fresh ginger

1 teaspoon chopped fresh garlic

2 teaspoons ground coriander

1½ teaspoons ground cardamom

1 teaspoon cayenne

1 teaspoon ground cumin

½ cinnamon stick

½ teaspoon turmeric

¼ teaspoon nutmeg

Score chicken breasts. Combine the tikka paste ingredients and rub on the chicken.

Combine the marinade ingredients. Soak the chicken in the marinade, refrigerated, overnight.

Remove the chicken from the marinade and wipe off excess. Reserve the marinade.

Preheat a skillet over medium heat. Add 1 tablespoon butter and sear chicken for 5-6 minutes on each side. Add the reserved marinade and bring to a simmer. Cover and simmer for 15 minutes, or until fully cooked. Stir in the remaining butter and lime juice. Sprinkle with cilantro.

Serve with basmati rice and roasted tomatoes and zucchini. Makes 4 servings.

Spicy Garlic Lime Chicken
Market Source

4 boneless, skinless chicken breasts

2 tablespoons butter

1 tablespoon olive oil

2 teaspoons garlic powder

5 tablespoons lime juice from Market Source limes

SPICE RUB

¾ teaspoon salt

¼ teaspoon ground black pepper

¼ teaspoon cayenne pepper

⅛ teaspoon paprika

¼ teaspoon garlic powder

⅛ teaspoon onion powder

¼ teaspoon dried thyme

¼ teaspoon dried parsley

Prepare the rub: In a small bowl, mix together salt, black pepper, cayenne, paprika, garlic powder, onion powder, thyme and parsley.

Sprinkle the rub generously on both sides of the chicken.

Heat butter and oil in a large, heavy skillet over medium heat. Add the chicken and sauté until golden brown, about 6 minutes on each side.

Sprinkle with garlic powder and lime juice. Cook for another 5 minutes, stirring frequently to coat evenly with sauce. Makes 4 servings.

Mushroom Marsala Chicken

Monterey Mushrooms/C&M Mushrooms/Giorgio Fresh Co.

½ cup olive oil, plus more for sautéing

1 cup chopped onion

3 tablespoons chopped garlic

16 ounces baby bella/crimini mushrooms, sliced (see note)

¾ cup all-purpose flour, divided

1½ teaspoons salt

Black pepper to taste

1 tablespoon Italian seasoning

2 pounds boneless, skinless chicken pieces

2½ cups Marsala wine (or chicken broth)

3 tablespoons fresh lemon juice

1 tablespoon sugar

1 tablespoon soy sauce

⅛ teaspoon Worcestershire sauce

1 teaspoon crushed red pepper flakes

⅓ cup chopped fresh basil

⅓ cup chopped fresh parsley

In a 12-inch skillet, heat a small amount of oil over medium heat. Sauté onion and garlic for about 2 minutes. Mix mushrooms with 2 tablespoons flour; add to the skillet and sauté until the mushrooms are heated through and the flour is lightly browned. Set aside.

Combine the remaining flour with salt, pepper and Italian seasoning; dredge chicken pieces. In another large skillet, heat ½ cup oil over medium heat. Brown the chicken pieces. Drain on paper towels and then add to the pan with the mushrooms.

Stir in Marsala, lemon juice, sugar, soy sauce, Worcestershire sauce and red pepper flakes. Simmer for 12 minutes. Stir in basil and parsley. Continue to simmer, uncovered, 10 minutes more, or until the chicken is cooked through.

Arrange the chicken on a platter; spoon the mushroom sauce on top. Serve with pasta, potatoes and/or vegetables. Makes 4 servings.

Note: White mushrooms can be used interchangeably with brown mushrooms.

Herb-Crusted Chicken Breasts with Tomato Provençal Sauce

Coleman Natural Foods

½ cup dry bread crumbs
2 teaspoons dried thyme
2 teaspoons dried basil
2 teaspoons dried oregano
½ cup all-purpose flour
2 organic whole eggs
¼ cup water
4 Coleman Organic boneless, skinless chicken breasts

¼ cup (or more) grated Asiago cheese

TOMATO PROVENÇAL SAUCE
2 tablespoons organic olive oil
1 organic onion, diced
1 teaspoon minced garlic
1 14.5-ounce can organic diced tomatoes

Preheat oven to 375°F. Line a rimmed baking sheet with foil.

In a large mixing bowl, combine bread crumbs with herbs and mix well. Place flour in a shallow bowl. In another bowl, mix eggs with water.

Place chicken breasts in the flour and dust completely. Dip the floured chicken into the egg wash, making sure it is completely coated. Then place in the herbed bread crumbs and cover completely. Place on the baking sheet and bake for 25 minutes, or until the internal temperature is 165°F.

Prepare the sauce: Heat oil in a sauté pan over medium-high heat. Add onion and cook until translucent, 5-6 minutes. Add garlic and cook for 30 seconds. Add tomatoes, cover and cook over low heat for 10 minutes.

When the chicken has finished cooking, preheat the oven broiler. Spoon the sauce over the chicken and sprinkle the cheese on top of that. Place under the broiler until the cheese has melted. Makes 4 servings.

FRANCE FREEMAN

MELANIE HOUSMAN
Costco Meat Buyer

Consumers may sometimes be confused by the terms "all natural" and "organic." The two are not interchangeable. A product can be called "all natural" if it does not contain artificial flavoring, coloring ingredients, chemical preservatives or other synthetic ingredients, and the product is minimally processed.

But to be organic, like Coleman Organic chicken, a product must meet a variety of criteria. Certified organic free-range chickens are:

• Fed a certified organic, all-vegetarian diet

• Raised without antibiotics

• Given no added hormones (federal regulations prevent the use of hormones in chicken)

• Certified by a third party to verify the way in which the chickens are raised

Coleman Organic chickens are certified by Oregon Tilth, a nonprofit research and education organization dedicated to environmentally sound agriculture.

The result is a preservative-free, free-range chicken that has an old-fashioned chicken taste.

Aztec Rotisserie Chicken Lasagna
GoodHeart Brand Specialty Foods

**Thick corn tortilla chips
or corn tortillas**

**3 cups Tomato and Chile
Sauce (see note)**

**½ pound hand-pulled meat
from a Kirkland Signature
rotisserie chicken**

1½ cups crema Mexicana

**1½ cups shredded Monterey
Jack or mild Cheddar**

TOMATO AND CHILE SAUCE

**3 14½-ounce cans diced
roasted tomatoes**

1 cup diced onion

4 teaspoons minced garlic

3 jalapeños, stems removed

2 tablespoons olive oil

**3 roasted poblano peppers,
peeled, seeded and diced**

Salt and pepper

Preheat oven to 350°F.

Prepare the sauce: In a blender, puree tomatoes, onion, garlic and jalapeños. Heat oil in a skillet over medium heat. Add the puree and cook until it thickens and becomes more orange in color. Add poblanos. Season to taste with salt and pepper.

Line a 9-by-9-inch baking dish with a layer of chips. Top with ¼ of the sauce, then ¼ of the chicken, ¼ of the crema and ¼ of the cheese. Repeat with 3 more layers, ending with cheese.

Cover and bake for 30 minutes. Uncover and bake for 10 minutes, or until browned. Makes 6 servings.

Note: Leftover sauce will keep, refrigerated, for about a week.

Turkey Casserole
Unilever

**4 cups leftover prepared
stuffing, divided**

**4 cups coarsely chopped
leftover cooked turkey
(about 1 pound)**

**¾ cup Hellmann's
or Best Foods Real
Mayonnaise, divided**

**¼ cup whole-berry
cranberry sauce**

**2 cups leftover
mashed potatoes**

**1½ cups shredded
mozzarella cheese
(about 6 ounces)**

**Dried cranberries,
for garnish (optional)**

Preheat oven to 375°F. Spray an 8-inch baking dish with nonstick cooking spray.

Spoon in 2 cups stuffing, then top with turkey.

Combine ¼ cup mayonnaise with cranberry sauce; spread evenly over the turkey.

In a large bowl, combine the remaining ½ cup mayonnaise, potatoes and cheese. Spread evenly on the turkey. Top with the remaining 2 cups stuffing.

Bake for 40 minutes, or until heated through. Let stand for 10 minutes before serving. Makes 6 servings.

Creamy Chicken Ramen with Spinach and Mushrooms
Nissin Top Ramen

- 1 tablespoon oil
- 1 cup boneless chicken breast cut into thin pieces
- ½ cup sliced mushrooms
- ½ small onion, diced
- 1 cup water
- ½ package (4 ounces) light cream cheese
- 1 3-ounce package Chicken Flavor Top Ramen
- 1 cup coarsely chopped spinach
- ¼ red bell pepper, thinly sliced
- ½ teaspoon coarsely ground black pepper

Heat oil in a skillet over medium heat. Add chicken and sauté until lightly browned. Remove from the pan and set aside.

Add mushrooms and onion to the pan and sauté until the onion is translucent.

Add water, cream cheese and the Top Ramen seasoning packet. Bring to a boil, stirring until the cream cheese has melted and the texture is smooth.

Add chicken, spinach, bell pepper and pepper; heat through.

As the mixture cooks, in a separate pot, boil 2 cups of water. Break noodles in half, add to the pot and cook for 3 minutes, stirring occasionally. Drain.

Toss noodles with the chicken mixture. Makes 2 servings.

Chicken with Pineapple Kimchi and Cantaloupe Yogurt
Chestnut Hill Farms/Legend Produce

- 4 boneless, skinless chicken breasts
- 1 tablespoon ground coriander
- 1 tablespoon ground cumin
- 2 garlic cloves, grated
- 4 tablespoons olive oil, divided
- ½ cantaloupe
- 1 cup couscous

PINEAPPLE KIMCHI
- 3 tablespoons grated ginger
- 3 tablespoons chopped garlic
- 1 tablespoon sugar
- 5 tablespoons Sriracha sauce
- 2 tablespoons sesame oil
- ½ cup soy sauce
- 1 pineapple, cut into chunks

CANTALOUPE YOGURT
- 1 tablespoon chopped mint
- 1 tablespoon chopped cilantro
- 1 cup diced cantaloupe
- 1-2 tablespoons cantaloupe juice
- 1 tablespoon chopped ginger
- 2 green onions, sliced
- Pinch of salt
- 6 ounces Greek yogurt

Prepare the kimchi: In a bowl, mix all ingredients. Let sit for 1 hour.

Preheat oven to 425°F. Rub chicken with mixture of coriander, cumin, garlic and 2 tablespoons oil. Bake for 50 minutes.

Prepare the yogurt: In a bowl, blend all ingredients.

Puree the ½ cantaloupe in a blender with ½ cup water. Cook in a saucepan until reduced by half.

Place couscous in a bowl and pour in the hot cantaloupe juice. Seal with plastic wrap for 10 minutes.

Heat 2 tablespoons oil in a frying pan over medium heat. Toast couscous until light brown.

Divide couscous among 4 plates. Slice each breast and place on couscous. Serve kimchi and yogurt on each side of chicken and couscous. Makes 4 servings.

Recipe developed by chef Aaron Arditti, Azul Restaurant at Mandarin Oriental.

Grilled Chicken Breasts with Pasta Caprese

Pilgrim's/Gold Kist Farms

1 cup olive oil

¼ cup white balsamic vinegar

Grated zest and juice of 1 lemon

1 teaspoon Dijon mustard

1 teaspoon chopped garlic

Salt and pepper

4 chicken breasts

12 ounces orecchiette pasta

1 pint baby mozzarella pearls

2 ounces Parmesan cheese, shaved

Combine oil, vinegar, lemon zest and juice, mustard, garlic, and salt and pepper to taste. Add chicken and marinate, refrigerated, for 2-8 hours.

PASTA SAUCE

1 cup dry white wine

2 cups chicken broth

Grated zest and juice of 1 lemon

1 tablespoon chopped garlic

2 pints small cherry tomatoes

4 tablespoons thinly sliced basil, divided

2 tablespoons chopped fresh parsley

1 tablespoon chopped fresh thyme

Preheat grill to medium-high. Grill chicken to 165°F, about 20 minutes. Cook pasta according to package directions.

Prepare the sauce: In a large sauté pan, cook wine over high heat until reduced by half. Add broth, lemon zest and juice, and garlic. Cook until reduced by half. Add tomatoes and 2 tablespoons basil, parsley, thyme, and salt and pepper to taste. Reduce heat to medium-high and cook until tomatoes are warm and skins begin to pop. Add pasta and mozzarella.

To serve, top with sliced chicken, basil and Parmesan. Makes 4 servings.

Roasted Garlic Chicken Sausage and Summer Vegetables
Classico

24 ounces al fresco Roasted Garlic Chicken Sausage (fully cooked)

1 pound penne rigate

2 tablespoons extra-virgin olive oil

1 cup thinly sliced Vidalia onion

2 garlic cloves, minced

1 cup sliced fresh mushrooms

1 large yellow bell pepper, thinly sliced

1 medium zucchini, cut in ¼-inch diagonal slices

3 cups Classico Tomato & Basil Pasta Sauce

Place sausages on an oiled grill rack set 4-5 inches over medium-low heat. Grill with the lid closed, turning frequently, for 7-9 minutes, or until the internal temperature is 165°F. Remove from the grill and keep warm.

Cook pasta al dente according to package directions. Drain, reserving ¼ cup of the pasta water. Keep warm.

Heat oil in a large nonstick sauté pan over medium heat. Sauté onion for 2 minutes. Add garlic and sauté for 1 minute. Add mushrooms, pepper and zucchini; sauté for 3-4 minutes. Add the reserved pasta water.

Cut the sausages into ¼-inch diagonal slices. Add to the vegetables and toss. Stir in tomato sauce and simmer for 3-4 minutes.

Divide the cooked penne among 8 bowls and top with the sauce. Makes 8 servings.

Tip: Serve with warm crusty Italian bread and shredded Parmesan.

Oxtail Ragu with Orecchiette
Cargill Meat Solutions

2¼ pounds Rumba oxtails

Salt and black pepper

All-purpose flour

¼ cup extra-virgin olive oil

1 yellow onion, cut in ¼-inch slices

2 cups dry white wine

½ cup chicken stock

1 cup tomato puree

1 tablespoon chopped fresh thyme

1 pound orecchiette, cooked

Preheat oven to 375°F.

Season oxtails with salt and pepper to taste. Dredge in flour and shake off any excess.

In a large heavy-bottomed cooking pot, heat oil until almost smoking. Add oxtails and sear the meat on all sides until it is a deep mahogany color. Remove and set aside.

Add onion to the pan and cook over high heat until golden. Add wine, stock, tomato puree, oxtails and thyme. Bring to a simmer, then cover and cook for approximately 1½ hours, or until the meat falls from the bone.

Remove the oxtails from the pan and remove the meat from the bones. Skim any fat from the surface of the sauce. Bring the sauce back to a simmer and add the oxtail meat. Simmer until it is a very thick ragu.

Serve with pasta. Makes 5 servings.

RUMBA®
Foods of the Soul® · Comidas del Alma®

Grilled Strip Steaks with Blue Cheese and Mushroom Gratin

JBS

2 tablespoons extra-virgin olive oil
1 cup quartered crimini mushrooms
½ cup diced yellow onion
½ cup diced white onion
2 tablespoons minced fresh garlic
¼ cup dry red or white wine
1 tablespoon rice wine vinegar

1 tablespoon soy sauce
1 teaspoon smoked paprika
1 cup diced blue cheese
¼ cup slivered fresh basil
4 New York strip steaks (8-12 ounces)
Salt and pepper
¼ cup dry bread crumbs

Heat oil in a sauté pan over medium heat. Sauté mushrooms and onions until caramelized. Add garlic and sauté another 2-3 minutes.

Deglaze the pan with wine. Add vinegar, soy sauce and smoked paprika. Reduce until the vegetables are lightly glazed. Chill the sauté. When cold, fold in blue cheese and basil.

Season steaks to taste with salt and pepper. Grill over hot coals, keeping in mind that they will be finished under the broiler. Preheat the oven broiler.

Spoon the gratin over the steaks and top with bread crumbs. Place under the broiler until the gratin is golden brown, about 2 minutes. Remove from the oven and serve immediately. Makes 4 servings.

Cinnamon Chile Crusted Steaks
McCormick

2 teaspoons McCormick Gourmet Collection ancho chile pepper

1½ teaspoons Kirkland Signature Saigon cinnamon

1½ teaspoons McCormick Gourmet Collection oregano leaves

1 teaspoon McCormick Gourmet Collection chipotle chile pepper

1 teaspoon McCormick Gourmet Collection parsley flakes

¾ teaspoon Kirkland Signature coarse-grind black pepper

½ teaspoon McCormick Gourmet Collection ground cumin

1¼ teaspoons salt

2 pounds New York strip or rib-eye steaks (1 inch thick)

Preheat the grill.

Mix all the seasonings on a plate.

Coat steaks evenly with the seasoning mixture.

Grill over medium-high heat for 6-8 minutes per side, or until cooked to taste. Makes 8 servings.

Nutritional information: Each serving has 255 calories, 38 g protein, 1 g carbohydrates, 11 g fat, 83 mg cholesterol, 1 g fiber, 445 mg sodium.

Latin-Spiced Rib Eye with Fire-Roasted Vegetables
Kirkland Signature/Tyson

4 Kirkland Signature 1-inch rib-eye steaks

4 zucchini, sliced

2 red bell peppers, sliced

1 teaspoon olive oil

Salt and pepper to taste

STEAK SPICE RUB

1 tablespoon salt

1½ teaspoons garlic powder

1½ teaspoons onion powder

2 tablespoons ancho powder

¾ teaspoon black pepper

CHIMICHURRI SAUCE

1 cup finely chopped fresh cilantro

2 teaspoons coarsely chopped fresh oregano

1 teaspoon finely chopped fresh garlic

1 tablespoon finely chopped yellow onion

½ cup olive oil

1½ tablespoons red wine vinegar

¼ teaspoon salt

¼ teaspoon ground black pepper

½ teaspoon red pepper flakes

Prepare the rub: Combine all ingredients. Season steaks with the rub and refrigerate for 30 minutes.

Toss the vegetables with oil, salt and pepper. Cover and refrigerate.

Prepare the sauce: Combine all ingredients. Cover and refrigerate.

Preheat the grill to medium-high.

Place the steaks and vegetables on the grill. Cook the steaks for 5-8 minutes on each side, or until cooked to taste. Cook the vegetables until tender.

Spoon the chimichurri sauce over the steaks or serve on the side. Makes 4 servings.

Lime Chipotle Skirt Steak Tacos with Corn Relish

National Beef

Juice and grated zest of 6 limes
¼ cup honey
¼ cup vegetable oil
¼ cup adobo sauce
2 teaspoons ground cumin
½ teaspoon ground black pepper
2½ pounds skirt steak,
 cut into 6 pieces
12 5- to 6-inch corn tortillas

CORN RELISH
12 green onions
4 ears of corn, husked
3 tablespoons olive oil, divided
Salt and pepper to taste
1 cup chopped fresh cilantro
2 teaspoons finely grated lime zest
2 tablespoons fresh lime juice
1 teaspoon chipotle chile powder

In a bowl, combine lime juice and zest, honey, oil, adobo sauce, cumin and pepper. Place steaks in a zip-lock bag and add marinade. Seal the bag and marinate in the refrigerator for 6-14 hours, turning occasionally.

Prepare the relish: Brush green onions and corn with 2 tablespoons oil and sprinkle with salt and pepper. Grill over medium-high heat until slightly charred, turning occasionally, about 2 minutes for onions and 7 minutes for corn. Cut corn kernels into a bowl. Add coarsely chopped green onions. Stir in cilantro, lime zest and juice, chipotle powder, 1 tablespoon oil, and salt and pepper.

Grill steaks over medium-high heat to an internal temperature of 145°F, about 5 minutes per side. Let rest for 5 minutes.

Place tortillas at the edge of the grill to warm, about 1 minute.

Arrange 2 warm tortillas on each plate. Thinly slice the steak across the grain. Divide the steak and juices among the tortillas. Spoon relish over each. Makes 6 servings.

Grilled Cilantro Lime Flank Steak with Tomato & Mint Couscous

Sandridge Foods/Rikki Rikki

1¼ pounds Kirkland Signature Cilantro-Lime marinated steak

3½ cups Sandridge Foods Tomato & Mint Couscous Salad

Fresh mint sprigs, for garnish

Set the grill on high and heat to 450°F.

Place the marinated meat on the grill and cook for 4 minutes on each side, or until cooked to taste. Remove the meat from the grill and let rest for 5 minutes.

After the meat has rested, slice on the bias with a sharp knife. Roll or fold up the slices of meat.

Place couscous salad on plates. Place the meat slices beside the salad.

Garnish the salad with a sprig of fresh mint. Makes 4 servings.

Grilled Roast Beef with Chimichurri and Sweet Potatoes

Cargill Meat Solutions

8 sweet potatoes

1 bunch Italian parsley

¼ cup fresh cilantro

3 garlic cloves

1 jalapeño, diced

¼ cup olive oil

¼ cup red wine vinegar

¼ cup fresh lime juice

1 1.5-pound package Morton's of Omaha Sliced Roast Beef

Preheat the grill to medium-hot.

Roast sweet potatoes on the grill until tender, about 40 minutes.

In a blender, combine parsley leaves, cilantro, garlic, jalapeño, oil, vinegar and lime juice. Puree the ingredients into a paste.

Warm sliced beef on the grill. Serve with the chimichurri sauce and roasted sweet potatoes. Makes 8 servings.

Slow-Cooker Chuck Roast
Lea & Perrins

3 pounds Certified Angus Beef chuck roast

Salt and pepper

1 48-ounce can beef broth

1 large onion, sliced, about 3 cups

1 cup Lea & Perrins Worcestershire sauce

½ cup Heinz tomato ketchup

Season roast with salt and pepper to taste. Place in a slow cooker.

Add the remaining ingredients. Set on low and cook for 8 hours, or until fork tender.

Gently remove the roast and cut or shred into bite-size pieces. Pour the sauce over the roast and serve. Makes 6 servings.

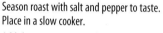

Herb-Roasted Top Round with Roasted Mushrooms and Sherry Sauce
Cargill Meat Solutions

1 4-pound choice top round roast

Diamond Crystal kosher salt

Black pepper

3 tablespoons extra-virgin olive oil

4 cups fresh bread crumbs

4 garlic cloves, minced

2 teaspoons chopped fresh thyme

2 tablespoons chopped fresh rosemary

¼ cup butter, melted

3 tablespoons Dijon mustard

2 pounds whole mushrooms

2 cups chicken stock

½ cup dry sherry

Preheat oven to 350°F.

Season the roast with salt and pepper to taste.

In a large pan, heat oil over medium-high heat. Add the roast and sear on all sides until it is mahogany brown. Transfer to a shallow roasting pan with a wire rack in the bottom.

In a bowl, combine bread crumbs, garlic, thyme, rosemary, melted butter and mustard. Place on top of the roast. Add mushrooms to the pan.

Place the roast in the oven. When the crust begins to brown, about 8-10 minutes, tent loosely with foil. Cook the roast for 1 hour, or until the internal temperature is 135°F.

Remove from the oven and let the meat rest for 15 minutes before slicing.

Add chicken stock and sherry to the pan and scrape up any roasting juices. Bring to a simmer and cook until reduced to a sauce consistency. Serve over sliced beef and roasted mushrooms. Makes 12 servings.

Roast Rib Eye and Herb Popovers
JBS

15- to 17-pound rib-eye roast

⅓ cup favorite steak seasoning
or ⅓ cup equal parts coarse salt
and coarsely ground pepper

HERB POPOVERS

3 large eggs

1½ cups flour

1½ cups whole milk

1½ tablespoons butter, melted

¾ teaspoon salt

2 tablespoons finely chopped fresh chives

½ teaspoon finely chopped fresh thyme

1 teaspoon chopped fresh parsley

Prepare the popover batter: In a blender, combine eggs, flour, milk, melted butter and salt. Blend until smooth. Strain into a small pitcher, cover and refrigerate for 4-28 hours.

Preheat oven to 425°F. Trim the roast of fat, leaving at least ¼ inch on the top side. Rub seasoning all over the roast. Place on a rack in a large shallow roasting pan. Roast in the oven for 20 minutes.

Reduce the heat to 350°F and roast for approximately 15-20 minutes per pound, or until the internal temperature is 140°F (medium-rare). Remove from the oven, cover with foil and let sit for 10-15 minutes before slicing.

Meanwhile, prepare the popovers: Preheat the oven to 425°F. Spoon ½ teaspoon of roast beef fat from the pan into each of 12 muffin cups. Place the pan in the oven and heat for 2½ minutes.

Add the herbs to the batter. Fill the muffin cups half full of batter. Bake for 15 minutes, then reduce the heat to 350°F and bake for another 15 minutes, or until golden brown. Makes 12 servings.

Shepherd's Pie with Organic Ground Beef

Organic Ranchers

4 large potatoes (preferably organic), peeled and cubed

1 tablespoon butter

1 tablespoon finely chopped white onion

½ cup shredded Cheddar cheese, divided

Salt and pepper

5 carrots, chopped

1 tablespoon olive oil

1 red onion, chopped

1 pound Kirkland Signature 85/15 organic ground beef

2 tablespoons all-purpose flour

1 tablespoon ketchup

1 teaspoon Dijon mustard

¾ cup beef broth

Bring a large pot of salted water to a boil. Add potatoes and cook until tender but still firm, about 15 minutes. Drain and mash. Mix in butter, white onion and ¼ cup cheese. Season to taste with salt and pepper. Set aside.

Bring a large pot of salted water to a boil. Add carrots and cook until tender but still firm, about 15 minutes. Drain and mash. Set aside.

Preheat oven to 375°F.

Heat oil in a large frying pan over medium heat. Add red onion and cook until translucent. Add ground beef and cook until well browned. Pour off excess fat, then stir in flour and cook for 1 minute. Add ketchup, mustard and beef broth. Bring to a boil, then reduce the heat and simmer for 5 minutes.

Spread the ground beef in an even layer on the bottom of a 2-quart casserole. Next, spread a layer of mashed carrots. Top with the mashed potato mixture and sprinkle with the remaining cheese.

Bake for 20 minutes, or until golden brown. Makes 4-5 servings.

The Katama Company

TINA MILLER

SCOTT LIVELY
Owner, Katama Company

I'm a big fan of the Kirkland Signature 1-pound organic beef blocks. I almost never make patties out of this ground beef: This is a cook's grind. In my home we use it to make Bolognese, tacos and one of my family's favorites, shepherd's pie. I also think the 85 percent beef-to-fat ratio is the perfect combination of flavor and low-fat benefits.

The packaging is convenient and allows for freezing one or two of the blocks if they're not to be used all at once. Also, they fold and fit nicely into the freezer.

Not only is this meat delicious, but each serving provides my family with high-quality protein, iron, zinc and B vitamins. And it feels good knowing that my family is eating organic beef that is free of added growth hormones and antibiotics.

Ground Beef and Tots Casserole
Kirkland Signature/Orleans International

- 2 pounds Kirkland Signature ground beef (85% lean or leaner)
- 1 tablespoon butter or margarine
- 1 onion, chopped
- 1 green bell pepper, chopped
- 1 10.75-ounce can condensed cream of mushroom or cream of chicken soup
- 1 soup can full of milk
- 1 2-pound package frozen potato tots, thawed

Preheat oven to 350°F. Grease a 2- or 2½-quart casserole.

In a sauté pan, brown beef over medium heat. Drain off the grease. Remove the beef from the pan and set aside.

In the same pan, melt butter. Add onions and bell pepper; sauté over medium heat until softened.

Return the beef to the pan, then add soup and milk. Stir to combine, and cook for a few minutes.

Line the bottom of the prepared casserole with half of the tots. Add the meat mixture in an even layer. Top with another layer of tots.

Bake for 45-60 minutes, or until the tots are browned and the meat mixture is bubbling. Makes 8 servings.

Tasty Chili Mac and Cheese
Kirkland Signature/Orleans International

- 2 pounds Kirkland Signature lean ground beef
- 1 1-ounce package chili seasoning (or make your own with chili powder and your favorite spices)
- 1 onion, chopped
- 1 teaspoon minced garlic
- 1 4-ounce can diced jalapeños
- 1 28-ounce can crushed tomatoes
- Salt and pepper
- 1 15-ounce can chili beans (optional)
- 1 pound seashell pasta (or elbow macaroni or penne)
- 1½ cups grated Cheddar or Monterey Jack cheese

In a medium-size pot or Dutch oven, brown ground beef over medium heat. Drain off excess fat.

Add chili seasoning to taste, onion, garlic, jalapeños and tomatoes and their juice. Simmer for 30 minutes over medium heat. Add water to keep a good consistency if needed. Season to taste with salt and pepper. Add beans.

Cook pasta according to package directions. Drain and rinse, then add to the mix and stir to combine.

Sprinkle grated cheese over the top and put the lid on the pot until the cheese has melted. Makes 6 servings.

Spiral Ham with Caramel Pecans and Bacon

Farmland Foods

1 Farmland Spiral-Sliced Ham half

1 pound Kirkland Signature hickory-smoked bacon, cut into ½-inch pieces

8 ounces chopped pecans

16 ounces caramel topping/sauce

½ cup packed light or dark brown sugar

Heat ham according to package directions.

Cook bacon in a large skillet over medium-high heat until crisp; remove from the pan and drain. Carefully pour all but ¼ cup bacon grease from the pan.

Add pecans to the pan. Reduce the heat to medium and cook, stirring, until the pecans are toasted. Stir in caramel topping, brown sugar and bacon. Cook and stir until the sugar has dissolved. Keep warm.

Remove the ham from the oven and place on a serving platter. Spoon the bacon mixture over the ham and between the slices. Makes about 16 servings.

Note: If desired, place the warm bacon mixture in a serving bowl for people to ladle over their own servings.

Black Forest Ham with Roasted Parsnips and Bourbon Pepper Glaze
Cargill Meat Solutions

¼ cup soy sauce

¼ cup maple syrup

3 tablespoons balsamic vinegar

4 garlic cloves, minced

2 teaspoons ground black pepper

¼ cup bourbon

1 1.75-pound package Kirkland Signature sliced Black Forest ham

3 pounds parsnips, peeled and halved

Preheat oven to 400°F.

In a saucepan, combine soy sauce, maple syrup, vinegar, garlic, pepper and bourbon. Cook over medium-high heat until reduced by half. Set aside.

Place sliced ham in a baking pan with the parsnips around the edges. Bake for 30 minutes, or until the ham is warmed through and the parsnips are tender.

Pour the glaze over the ham and parsnips and return to the oven for 10 minutes. Serve immediately. Makes 8 servings.

Pizzaaa SPAM Bake
Hormel Foods

1 16-ounce package elbow macaroni

1 12-ounce can SPAM Less Sodium, cubed

1 cup diced Hormel pepperoni

1 onion, chopped

1 16-ounce jar pizza sauce

4 cups shredded mozzarella cheese, divided

5 teaspoons grated Parmesan or Romano cheese

Preheat oven to 350°F.

Cook macaroni according to package directions and drain.

In a skillet over medium heat, cook SPAM, pepperoni and onion until lightly browned.

In a large bowl, combine cooked macaroni, the SPAM mixture and pizza sauce. Slowly stir in 3 cups mozzarella.

Place the mixture in a casserole. Sprinkle with the remaining mozzarella and the Parmesan. Bake for 45 minutes, or until thoroughly heated and the cheese is melted. Makes 6 servings.

Apple Pear Maple Pork Chops
Kingsburg Orchards

APPLE PEARS

4 tablespoons butter, divided

1 small to medium onion, cut in ¼-inch slivers

3-4 Kingsburg Orchards apple pears, cut in ⅛-inch slivers

¼ cup maple syrup

2 tablespoons dark brown sugar

½ teaspoon kosher salt

½ teaspoon ground black pepper

PORK CHOPS

1 teaspoon kosher salt

½ teaspoon ground black pepper

½ teaspoon fresh thyme (or dried)

4-6 boneless thick-cut pork chops

1 tablespoon extra-virgin olive oil

⅓ cup apple juice or broth of your choice

Prepare the apple pears: In a small deep skillet, melt 2 tablespoons butter over medium-low heat. Add onion and sauté until translucent and tender, about 5-7 minutes.

Add apple pear slices and the remaining 2 tablespoons butter. Continue to cook, stirring frequently, until the apple pears are tender, about 7-10 minutes.

Add maple syrup, brown sugar, salt and pepper. Continue cooking until very tender and golden brown.

Prepare the pork chops: Preheat oven to 350°F. Grease a 13-by-9-inch baking dish.

Combine salt, pepper and thyme, and season the pork chops.

Heat oil in a sauté pan over medium-high heat. Add the pork chops and sear on all sides.

Transfer to the baking dish. Pour in apple juice or broth. Cover with foil and bake for 10-15 minutes.

Pour the apple pear mixture over the pork chops and bake, uncovered, for 10 more minutes, or until the internal temperature is 160°F.

Serve immediately. Makes 4-6 servings.

Tip: The key to cooking this dish is to have the apple pears ready in advance. If the pork chops sit too long in the oven, they will dry out.

Pan-Roasted Pork Loin Chops with Apricot-Cheddar Stuffing, Serrano Ham and Brown Sugar Glaze
JBS/Swift Premium

4 boneless pork loin chops (8-12 ounces)

8 thin slices serrano ham

BROWN SUGAR GLAZE

1 cup light brown sugar

½ cup root beer

½ cup rice wine vinegar

½ cup soy sauce

1 star anise pod

1 cinnamon stick

2 bay leaves

STUFFING

1 cup diced dried apricots

½ cup diced dried figs

1 cup cubed English Cheddar

2 tablespoons minced fresh chives

1 tablespoon minced scallions

1 teaspoon garlic powder

1 teaspoon Chinese five-spice powder

Salt and pepper to taste

Prepare the glaze: In a saucepan, combine all ingredients and cook over medium heat until reduced to a syrup. Strain and keep warm.

Prepare the stuffing: In a bowl, combine all ingredients.

Preheat oven to 400°F.

Make a slit through the side of each chop to form a pocket. Fill the pocket with stuffing and season both sides with salt and pepper.

Wrap each chop with 2 slices of ham so the stuffing is completely covered.

Heat a medium cast-iron or ovenproof skillet in the oven.

Place the chops in the skillet and roast until seared on one side, 5-10 minutes. Flip the chops and roast for 5-10 minutes, or until evenly browned and the internal temperature is 145°F at the thickest part of the meat.

Serve with brown sugar glaze. Makes 4 servings.

Sautéed Pork Loin with Grapes
Four Star Fruit

4 ½-inch-thick slices of boneless pork loin, about 1 pound

Flour seasoned to taste with salt and pepper, for dredging

2 tablespoons olive oil

2 tablespoons minced shallots

1 cup Four Star Fruit green and red seedless grapes, cut in half

2 tablespoons Cognac

2 tablespoons chopped fresh tarragon

1 cup canned chicken broth

2 teaspoons firmly packed dark brown sugar

1 tablespoon Dijon mustard

Dredge pork in seasoned flour and shake off excess. Heat oil in a large skillet over medium heat. Add the pork and brown on both sides. Using tongs, transfer the pork to a platter. Reduce the heat to low and add shallots and grapes. Sauté for 3 minutes, stirring occasionally.

Add Cognac and tarragon; simmer until almost all the liquid evaporates. Add chicken broth and brown sugar; boil the mixture until the liquid is reduced by half.

Add the pork and juices to the pan and cook for about 5 minutes. Remove the pork and transfer to a serving platter or plates.

Turn off the heat and whisk mustard into the sauce until well blended. Season to taste with salt and pepper. Pour the sauce over the pork and serve. Makes 2 servings.

Chipotle-Dijon Ribs
Farmland Foods

½ cup packed light or dark brown sugar
1 tablespoon salt
2 teaspoons chipotle chile powder
1 teaspoon garlic powder

1 teaspoon smoked paprika
4 pounds Farmland St. Louis-Style Pork Ribs
½ cup Dijon mustard
Barbecue sauce (optional)

In a small bowl, combine sugar, salt, chile powder, garlic powder and paprika; mix well.

Coat ribs on all sides with mustard. Sprinkle heavily with the seasoning blend.

Cover and refrigerate for 8-24 hours. Preheat oven to 350°F.

Place the ribs on a foil-lined shallow baking pan. Roast for 1½-2 hours, or until tender. During the last 30 minutes, brush the ribs with barbecue sauce if desired. Makes 4 servings.

Grilled Lamb Chops with Warm Couscous Salad and Spinach

JBS Australia

¼ cup (2 ounces) wheat berries

8 lamb chops

¼ cup (2 ounces) large pearl couscous

2 tablespoons olive oil, divided

½ bunch green onions, sliced thin

½ red bell pepper, cut in small dice

1 yellow squash, zucchini and carrot, cut in small dice

4 teaspoons finely chopped garlic, divided

Salt and pepper

20 ounces spinach

In a saucepan, cover wheat berries with 4 cups of water and boil over medium-high heat for 2 hours, or until tender; drain.

VINAIGRETTE

3 ounces Champagne or white balsamic vinegar

1 tablespoon Dijon mustard

Grated zest and juice of 1 lemon

½ teaspoon salt

¼ teaspoon pepper

1 tablespoon chopped fresh dill

1 tablespoon chopped fresh parsley

1 teaspoon chopped fresh thyme

2 teaspoons finely chopped garlic

5 ounces olive oil

Prepare the vinaigrette: In a mixer, combine vinegar, mustard, lemon zest and juice, salt, pepper, herbs and garlic. On medium-high speed, slowly drizzle in oil. Marinate lamb in ⅓ of the vinaigrette for 2 hours.

Cook couscous in boiling water for 8 minutes; drain. Preheat the grill to medium-high. Grill lamb for about 6 minutes per side. Heat 1 tablespoon oil in a sauté pan over medium-high heat. Sauté diced vegetables and 2 teaspoons garlic for 2-3 minutes. Add wheat berries, couscous, ⅓ of vinaigrette, and salt and pepper. Remove from the pan. Add 1 tablespoon oil to the pan; sauté spinach and remaining garlic. Season with salt and pepper.

Place some spinach on each plate. Top with warm salad. Prop a lamb chop on either side. Drizzle with vinaigrette. Makes 4 servings.

Grilled Lamb Chops

T & R Pastoral Company/Foodcomm Fresh and Natural

¼ cup minced shallots
2 tablespoons minced garlic
2 tablespoons onion powder
2 tablespoons garlic powder
¼ cup salt

2 tablespoons ground black pepper
3 tablespoons chopped fresh rosemary
3 tablespoons chopped fresh thyme
2-3 frenched Australian racks of lamb, cut into chops

In a bowl, combine the first 8 ingredients.

Coat lamb chops with the seasoning mixture and let sit for 24 hours in the refrigerator.

On a hot grill, cook the lamb chops to taste (for medium, an internal temperature of 140°F). Makes 4-6 servings.

Recipe developed by chef Marty Cattaneo and Dio Deka Restaurant.

Grilled Butterflied Leg of Lamb
JBS Australia

4-5 pounds boneless leg of lamb

2 tablespoons thinly sliced fresh garlic

1½ tablespoons salt

2 teaspoons freshly ground black pepper

2-3 tablespoons chopped fresh rosemary

½ cup olive oil

2 cups dry red wine

4 long metal skewers

Cut lamb so it lies flat with the skin side out. It should all be about the same thickness.

In a large resealable bag, combine garlic, salt, pepper, rosemary, oil and wine; mix well. Add the lamb to the bag, seal and refrigerate for 2-4 hours.

Preheat the grill to medium.

Remove the lamb from the marinade and lay flat on a cutting board with the cut side up. Discard the remaining marinade.

Insert 2 skewers 2-3 inches apart from right to left through the center of the meat. Insert the other 2 skewers from front to back to hold in any loose pieces and stabilize.

Grill over medium heat to an internal temperature of 140°F (medium-rare). Remove to a platter and let rest under foil for 20-30 minutes before slicing. Makes 12-15 servings.

Richie's Mini Pot Roast Burger
Labriola Baking Company

1 medium gold potato

Sea salt, ground black pepper and thyme

Olive oil

½ medium yellow onion, peeled

3 tablespoons butter, divided

3 ounces ground beef

1 ounce Tillamook extra-sharp white Cheddar, sliced or shredded

2 ounces Morton's cooked beef pot roast, sliced

1 Labriola Pretzel Slider Bun

Preheat oven to 350°F.

Cut potato into ¼-inch slices. Season to taste with salt, pepper and thyme. Lightly coat with oil. Place potato in a baking dish, then bake until tender and golden, about 20 minutes.

Cut onion into ¼-inch slices. Sauté over medium heat in 2 tablespoons butter, stirring frequently, until soft and caramel colored, about 15 minutes.

When the potato and onion are done, keep them warm.

Shape ground beef into a patty. Season to taste with salt and pepper. Pan-fry with the remaining butter, or grill. Top with cheese and melt.

Warm the sliced pot roast.

Slice the bun and toast slightly in the skillet or on the grill.

To serve, place the burger on the bun. Top with potato, pot roast and onion. Makes 1 serving.

Mediterranean Club Sandwich

Sabra

3 slices whole-grain, sourdough
  or ciabatta bread, toasted

2 tablespoons Sabra Roasted Pine
  Nut Hummus

2 ounces sliced turkey breast

1¼ ounces (about 2 tablespoons)
  roasted red pepper

1 ounce thinly sliced prosciutto
  or cooked bacon

2-3 teaspoons chopped
  Kalamata olives

4 frill picks or toothpicks, for serving

SALAD

½ cup baby arugula

5 fresh basil leaves, chopped

½ teaspoon lemon juice

1 teaspoon olive oil

⅛ teaspoon ground sumac (optional)

Salt to taste

Prepare the salad: Combine all ingredients and toss to coat. Set aside.

To assemble the sandwich, lay bread slices side by side. Spread hummus on each slice. Top one slice with turkey and roasted red pepper. Top the second with prosciutto (or bacon), salad and olives. Combine the three layers to create a club sandwich.

Insert a frill pick or toothpick in each quarter. Slice the sandwich into quarters, creating 4 triangles. Makes 1 serving.

Tip: Serve with Greek olives and a tabouli salad for a sunny Mediterranean lunch.

Asiago Bagel Club Sandwiches

Einstein Brothers Bagels/Noah's New York Bagels

Leaf lettuce or romaine, to taste

2 tomatoes

Sea salt and pepper

1 ripe avocado

4 Kirkland Signature Asiago cheese bagels

1 tablespoon Dijon mustard, or to taste

16 ounces oven-roasted turkey, thinly sliced

4 slices Swiss cheese

8 strips thick-cut bacon, cooked crisp

1 tablespoon light mayonnaise, or to taste

Wash lettuce and dry the leaves. Slice tomatoes, then lightly salt and pepper. Peel avocado, remove the seed and cut each half into 4 slices.

Cut each bagel into 3 horizontal slices. Grill or toast the bagel slices.

On the bottom layer of each bagel, lightly spread mustard. Add 4 ounces of turkey and a slice of cheese. Place the middle bagel slice on top. Add lettuce, then tomato slices, 2 slices of bacon and 2 avocado slices. Spread mayo on the inside of the top bagel layer. Close the sandwich. Makes 4 servings.

Savory Tomato Monte Cristo Sandwiches with Pepper Slaw

BC Hot House Foods, Inc./The Oppenheimer Group

4 sandwich-size slices Swiss cheese

2 large beefsteak tomatoes, thinly sliced

Fresh basil leaves (optional)

8 slices bread

5 large eggs

3 tablespoons half-and-half (or milk)

1 teaspoon salt

1 teaspoon pepper

2 tablespoons chopped fresh chives

Butter (or oil), for frying

Spicy ketchup, for serving (see note)

PEPPER SLAW

¼ cup red wine vinegar

1 tablespoon sugar

2 tablespoons olive oil

Dash of hot sauce (to taste)

Salt and pepper

3 sweet bell peppers (red, yellow or orange), julienned

½ sweet onion, sliced in thin strips

Assemble the sandwiches by placing 1 cheese slice, 2-3 tomato slices and basil leaves (if desired) on 4 slices of bread. Top with remaining bread slices.

In a bowl, beat together eggs, half-and-half, salt, pepper and chives.

Place butter (or oil) in a skillet and heat to medium-high. Dip the bread into the egg mixture to coat and place in the heated skillet. Fry for 3-4 minutes per side, or until the bread is crisp and golden brown.

Serve with the slaw and spicy ketchup. Makes 4 servings.

Note: To make your own spicy ketchup, add 1 minced garlic clove, a dash of Worcestershire sauce and hot sauce to taste to ½ cup of ketchup. These sandwiches are also great with chipotle sauce.

Prepare the slaw: In a large bowl, whisk together vinegar, sugar, oil, hot sauce, and salt and pepper to taste. Add peppers and onions; toss to blend. Set aside.

expect the world from us

Cheesy Turkey Monte Cristo Sandwiches
Kirkland Signature/Michael Foods

1¼ cups AllWhites or Better'n Eggs

¼ cup low-fat milk

¼ teaspoon ground nutmeg

Freshly ground pepper to taste

8 slices rye or whole-wheat bread

¼ cup Dijon mustard

1 8-ounce package Crystal Farms Wisconsin Sharp Cheddar or Havarti Deli Slices

8 ounces sliced smoked turkey

1 medium ripe pear or apple, cored and thinly sliced

2 tablespoons olive oil or butter, divided

Warm maple syrup or apple butter, for serving

In a shallow dish, lightly beat AllWhites or Better'n Eggs, milk, nutmeg and pepper with a fork.

On a work surface, lay out bread slices. Spread with mustard. Top 4 pieces of bread with 1 slice cheese, turkey, pear slices and remaining slices of cheese. Top with the remaining bread slices, mustard-side down.

Heat 1 tablespoon oil in a large skillet over medium heat. Dip 2 sandwiches in the egg mixture, coating both top and bottom. Place in the skillet and cook for 5 minutes, or until the bottoms are browned. Carefully turn over and cook 4 minutes longer, or until golden brown. Heat remaining oil and repeat with the remaining sandwiches.

Serve with syrup or apple butter. Makes 4 servings.

Cheesy Mac and Rib Melt
Tillamook

8 cups prepared macaroni and cheese

3 tablespoons Tillamook unsalted butter

4 yellow onions, cut in ¼-inch strips

2 cups barbecue sauce

4 cups prepared pulled pork

16 slices buttermilk bread

24 slices Tillamook Sharp Cheddar Cheese

SPREAD

¾ cup (6 ounces) Tillamook unsalted butter, at room temperature

¾ cup mayonnaise

Prepare the spread: Beat butter and mayonnaise until well mixed.

Spread warm macaroni and cheese on a sheet pan in a ¾-inch-thick layer. When cool, cut into squares slightly smaller than the bread slices.

In a sauté pan, melt 3 tablespoons butter over medium heat. Add onions and cook, stirring often, until caramelized, about 25 minutes. Do not brown.

In a saucepan, heat barbecue sauce. Add pork and simmer for 5 minutes.

Preheat a griddle to 350°F.

Butter one side of bread slices with spread. On the other side of 8 slices, lay 1 slice of cheese, 1 square of macaroni and cheese, then another slice of cheese. Add pork and onions. Top with a cheese slice and another slice of bread, buttered side out.

Slowly cook all sandwiches on the griddle until golden brown on both sides. To cook faster, place a bacon press on top of the sandwiches. Makes 8 servings.

Note: If the griddle heat is too high it will burn the bread. If the bread browns before the inside becomes hot, place sandwiches in the oven at 450°F to finish cooking.

Recipe courtesy of Dave Danhi and the Grilled Cheese Truck, Los Angeles.

Cashew Chicken Salad Sandwiches

Ann's House of Nuts/Harvest Manor Farms

2 cups diced cooked chicken

½ cup chopped Kirkland Signature salted cashews

½ cup chopped red apple

½ cup chopped peeled cucumber

½ cup mayonnaise

½ teaspoon sugar

½ teaspoon salt

Dash of pepper

6 lettuce leaves (optional)

6 kaiser rolls or croissants, split

In a large bowl, combine chicken, cashews, apple and cucumber.

In a small bowl, combine mayonnaise, sugar, salt and pepper. Add to the chicken mixture and toss to coat. Place a lettuce leaf and ½ cup chicken salad on each roll or croissant. Makes 6 servings.

Roasted Turkey Salad Sandwiches with Chipotle Mayo and Avocado on Whole Grain
La Brea Bakery

3 cups shredded roasted turkey (without skin)

8 slices La Brea Bakery Whole Grain Bread

2 cups watercress, arugula or baby greens

1 ripe avocado, peeled and sliced

Sea salt

CHIPOTLE MAYONNAISE

1 cup mayonnaise

¼ cup chopped fresh cilantro

2 tablespoons olive oil

2 tablespoons fresh lemon juice, or to taste

4 large garlic cloves, grated or minced

1½ teaspoons pureed or finely chopped chipotle peppers in adobo sauce

1 teaspoon kosher salt, or to taste

Prepare the chipotle mayonnaise: Combine all ingredients and mix thoroughly with a whisk. Add more salt and lemon juice to taste.

Place the shredded turkey in a bowl and toss with ¾ cup of the chipotle mayonnaise (use more or less depending on individual preference).

For each sandwich, place some turkey salad on a slice of bread. Place greens on the salad and top with slices of avocado. Add salt to taste and close the sandwich. Makes 4 servings.

LA BREA BAKERY

Bacon Cheeseburger Pizza
Kirkland Signature

12 ounces ground beef, cooked and seasoned to taste

1 Kirkland Signature frozen cheese pizza

5 slices bacon, cooked, cut in half

4 tablespoons ketchup

3 tablespoons yellow mustard

2 ounces iceberg lettuce, shredded

1 large vine-ripened tomato, thinly sliced

½ small yellow onion, diced

⅓ cup chopped dill pickles

Spread ground beef evenly over the pizza.

Arrange bacon pieces on the pizza.

Bake the pizza according to package directions.

When the pizza is cooked, remove from the oven. Squirt ketchup and mustard evenly over the pizza.

Evenly distribute the shredded lettuce over the pizza. Add tomatoes, onions and pickles. Makes 8 servings.

Spicy Southwest Beef Torta

La Brea Bakery

2½ pounds boneless beef chuck
 pot roast
1 white onion, sliced
1 can (about 14 ounces) beef broth
6 La Brea Bakery Torta Sandwich Rolls
¾ cup refried beans
1½ cups finely shredded sharp
 Cheddar cheese
1 white onion, thinly sliced
2 avocados, peeled, seeded and sliced

ANCHO CHILE MAYONNAISE
½ teaspoon dried ancho chile powder
¾ cup mayonnaise

CHIPOTLE DRESSING
2 chipotle peppers in adobo sauce,
 finely chopped
¼ cup olive oil
¼ cup fresh lime juice
¼ cup white vinegar
¼ cup chopped fresh cilantro
1 tablespoon minced garlic

Place pot roast and onion in a large pot. Add beef broth. Bring to a boil, then reduce the heat, cover tightly and simmer until the beef is fork-tender, about 3 hours. Remove the beef from the cooking liquid and let cool slightly. Strain the cooking liquid and skim off the fat; set aside. Trim and discard fat from the beef. Shred the beef with 2 forks. Combine the shredded beef with ½ cup cooking liquid and keep warm.

Prepare the mayonnaise: In a small bowl, combine both ingredients and blend.

Prepare the dressing: In a small bowl, combine all ingredients and blend.

Spread the bottom half of each sandwich roll with refried beans. Spread the other half with ancho chile mayonnaise. Spoon about ⅔ cup of the hot meat mixture onto each roll and drizzle with chipotle dressing. Add cheese, onion slices and avocados. Close the sandwich. If desired, serve the remaining cooking liquid as a dipping sauce. Makes 6 servings.

Tip: The recipe can be prepared using 2 packages (17 ounces each) refrigerated fully cooked pot roast or roast beef au jus. Prepare according to package directions, then shred the beef and combine with ½ cup gravy or au jus.

La Brea Bakery

Grilled Tex-Mex Chicken Torta

La Brea Bakery

4 cups shredded cooked chicken
(about 1 rotisserie chicken)

1 10-ounce can diced tomatoes
with green chilies, drained

1 cup mayonnaise

¾ cup chopped fresh cilantro

1 tablespoon minced garlic

Salt and pepper

6 La Brea Bakery Torta Sandwich Rolls

3 poblano chiles, roasted, peeled,
seeded and cut into strips (see note)

1 large white onion, cut into ¼-inch
slices, roasted (see note)

2 cups shredded Monterey Jack cheese

In a large bowl, combine chicken, tomatoes, mayonnaise, cilantro and garlic, mixing lightly but thoroughly. Season to taste with salt and pepper.

Spoon about ¾ cup of the chicken mixture onto the bottom half of each sandwich roll. Top evenly with poblano strips, onion slices and cheese. Close the sandwiches.

Grill the sandwiches in a panini press, on medium-high heat, until the torta roll is toasted and the cheese is melted, about 2 minutes. Makes 6 servings.

Note: To roast poblanos and onions, preheat oven to 400°F. Place whole poblanos and onion slices on a baking sheet. Roast for 20 minutes, or until the onions are tender and the poblano skins are blistered.

Tip: The sandwiches can also be grilled in a skillet over medium heat, turning once, until the roll is toasted and cheese is melted.

LA BREA BAKERY

Peanut Butter, Blueberry and Strawberry Sandwiches

Andrew & Williamson/Curry & Company/Gourmet Trading Company

12 ounces strawberries, rinsed and trimmed
8 ounces blueberries, rinsed and drained
2 cups peanut butter
12 slices bread
¼ cup honey or confectioners' sugar (optional)
Food picks, for serving

Cut 16 strawberry slices for garnish; set aside. Chop the remaining strawberries into ¼-inch pieces. Reserve 16 blueberries for garnish.

Spread ¾ of the peanut butter on the bread.

Arrange about ¼ cup blueberries on each of 4 slices, leaving small spaces between. Press gently into the peanut butter.

Add some chopped strawberries to the 4 slices, filling in the spaces. Drizzle with some of the honey or sprinkle with sugar if desired.

Place 4 bread slices, peanut-butter side down, on top of the 4 slices with berries. Spread with the remaining peanut butter. Repeat the layering with berries and honey or sugar.

Top with the final 4 slices of bread, peanut butter side down. Slice into quarter sandwiches and top with picks and reserved berries for garnish. Makes 4-6 servings.

Recipe developed by Christine W. Jackson, food stylist.

Albacore Waldorf Wraps
Kirkland Signature

1 7-ounce can Kirkland Signature solid white albacore tuna, drained and flaked

¼ cup plain Greek-style yogurt

1 teaspoon honey

¼ teaspoon curry powder

¼ cup walnuts, chopped

¼ cup diced celery

2 12-inch spinach-flavored tortilla wraps

2 cups fresh spinach leaves, washed and drained

1 Gala apple, cored and sliced (about 8 wedges)

In a small bowl, gently combine tuna, yogurt, honey, curry powder, walnuts and celery. Set aside.

On each tortilla, layer spinach leaves, apple wedges and tuna mixture. Roll tightly burrito-style and cut in half diagonally. Makes 2 servings.

Turkey and Dried Plum Pita Pockets
Kirkland Signature/Sunsweet

2 cups (about 12 ounces) diced cooked turkey or chicken

¾ cup (about 5 ounces) Kirkland Signature/ Sunsweet dried plums, chopped

½ cup sliced celery

½ cup plain nonfat yogurt

¼ cup sliced green onions

1 tablespoon sweet or hot mustard

Salt and pepper

6 lettuce leaves

3 whole-wheat pita breads, halved

In a medium bowl, combine turkey, dried plums, celery, yogurt, green onions and mustard. Blend until thoroughly mixed. Season to taste with salt and pepper. Store, covered, in the refrigerator for up to 3 days.

To serve, place 1 lettuce leaf in each pita pocket. Spoon ½ cup of the turkey mixture into each pita pocket. Makes 3-6 servings.

Fancy Parisian Wraps
Ready Pac

½ cup mayonnaise

2 tablespoons Dijon mustard

2½ teaspoons ground black pepper

½ teaspoon dried thyme

¼ teaspoon salt

1 16-ounce bag Ready Pac Grand Parisian Complete Salad Kit

8 12-inch white or whole-wheat tortillas, or lavash wraps

16 ounces sliced provolone cheese

8 ounces sliced turkey breast

8 ounces sliced ham

1 small red onion, thinly sliced

Combine mayonnaise, mustard, pepper, thyme and salt. Set aside and let stand.

Meanwhile, place salad greens from the salad kit in a large salad bowl. Drizzle with dressing from the salad kit and toss well. Combine with frosted almonds, cranberries and feta from the salad kit. Set aside.

Microwave 2-3 tortillas at a time between 2 damp paper towels, 15-20 seconds, or until heated through. Keep warm. Lay the tortillas on a wooden surface. Spread each tortilla with about 1 tablespoon of the mayonnaise mixture, leaving a 1-inch border.

Layer each wrap with 2 slices of provolone and 2 slices of turkey or ham, or 1 slice of each. Top each with about 1 cup of the salad mixture. Add equal portions of onion.

Fold in 1 inch on 2 opposite sides of each wrap, then roll up tightly, burrito style, from the bottom up. Wrap each tightly in waxed paper or plastic wrap. Slice in half or in 2-inch pieces on a bias. Makes 8-10 servings.

Chicken Fajitas

Mr. Yoshida's

2 tablespoons oil

1 medium onion, julienne sliced

1 medium green bell pepper, julienne sliced

1 medium red bell pepper, julienne sliced

1 pound boneless, skinless chicken breasts (about 3)

¾ cup Mr. Yoshida's Original Gourmet Sauce

8 flour tortillas, warmed

Heat oil in a wok or skillet until hot. Add onion and bell peppers; sauté until just soft, about 2 minutes. Remove with a slotted spoon to a plate and set aside.

Cut chicken into ½-inch-thick strips and sauté in the same pan for about 5 minutes, or until the chicken is no longer pink and internal temperature is 165°F. Return the vegetables to the pan along with the sauce and cook until the sauce comes to a boil and thickens. Remove the pan from the heat.

Spoon the chicken and vegetable mixture into warmed tortillas, roll up and serve. Makes 8 servings.

Tip: Salsa, sour cream and guacamole are nice accompaniments.

Chipotle Chicken Caesar Salad Wraps

Ventura Foods

1 20.5-ounce Kirkland Signature Chicken Caesar Salad Kit

½ cup diced fresh tomato

2 Flatout Traditional Flatbreads

CHIPOTLE CREAM CHEESE SPREAD

4 ounces cream cheese, softened

1-2 tablespoons chopped canned chipotle pepper in adobo sauce (see note)

2 tablespoons finely chopped pimientos

1 tablespoon finely chopped onion

1½ teaspoons chopped chives

Prepare the spread: Using an electric mixer, combine all ingredients and beat on high until the mixture is light and fluffy. If this is not being used right away, it can be refrigerated, covered, for 2-3 days.

In a kitchen bowl, combine the salad kit ingredients and diced tomato. Add the dressing and toss to coat.

Lay out flatbreads on a clean cutting board. Place half of the chipotle cream cheese on each flatbread and spread evenly.

Place an equal amount of the salad on one end of each flatbread. Roll the flatbread over the salad mixture, making a tube/sandwich wrap. Slice in half. Makes 2 servings.

Note: Don't use too much of the adobo sauce, as it will make the spread too runny.

Tip: These can also be sliced into small pinwheels for a party platter.

Hot Pop Pies

West Liberty Foods

1 14.1-ounce package refrigerated
  pie dough (2 crusts)

1 egg

18 ounces deli sliced meat and cheese,
  plus ¼ cup mustard (from a 5-pound
  Kirkland Signature Meat and Cheese
  Platter with Spicy Brown Mustard)

Preheat oven to 375°F.

Roll 1 piece of the dough into an 11-inch square. Cut into 6 rectangles, slicing the dough once crosswise and twice at equal intervals in the opposite direction.

Beat egg with 1 teaspoon water in a small bowl. Lightly brush along all edges of the rectangles.

Place 3 ounces of meat and cheese along the center of 3 of the dough rectangles, leaving ½ inch free around the edges. Top with the remaining 3 rectangles.

Egg-wash the sides together. Seal the edges using the tines of a fork. Place on a large ungreased baking sheet.

Repeat with the remaining dough, meat and cheese.

Brush the tops lightly with the remaining egg wash. Do not pierce the dough. Bake for 15-20 minutes, or until golden brown on top.

Serve with mustard and/or other prepared dipping sauces such as Thousand Island dressing or marinara sauce. Makes 6 servings.

WLF West Liberty Foods.

Desserts

Cherry-Peach Wonton Cups with Lemon-Mascarpone Cream
Stemilt Growers

1 Stemilt peach, pitted, peeled and diced (1 cup)

20-30 Stemilt cherries, pitted and halved (1½ cups)

1 teaspoon superfine granulated sugar

1 cup heavy whipping cream

½ cup confectioners' sugar, plus 3 tablespoons for dusting

8 ounces mascarpone cheese

1 tablespoon grated lemon zest

12 wonton wrappers (3½ inches square)

2 tablespoons unsalted butter, melted

Special equipment: 24-cup mini muffin tin

Preheat oven to 350°F.

Place fruit in a bowl. Sprinkle with superfine sugar and mix to blend. Set aside.

Place cream and ½ cup confectioners' sugar in the bowl of a stand mixer; beat on medium-low for 30-60 seconds. Increase the speed to medium-high and beat until the whip leaves a slight trail, 30-60 seconds. Increase the speed to high and beat until soft peaks form, 30-60 seconds. Transfer the cream to a clean bowl and set aside.

Put mascarpone in the bowl of the mixer (no rinsing necessary) and whip on medium-high for 30 seconds. Gently fold in the whipped cream with a spatula, combining without deflating. Return the bowl to the mixer, add lemon zest and mix on medium for about 15 seconds. Cover with plastic wrap and refrigerate.

Meanwhile, brush both sides of a wonton wrapper with melted butter. Gently place in a muffin cup, carefully pressing the center into the mold and pleating the sides to fit (corner tips should slightly fan). Repeat the process, placing a wrapper in every other cup to prevent overcrowding.

Bake for 5-8 minutes, or until slightly browned. Remove from the oven and set aside to cool for 2 minutes, then transfer the cups to a cooling rack. Once cooled, generously dust with confectioners' sugar.

Spoon 1-2 teaspoons of lemon-mascarpone cream into each cup, then top with 5-8 pieces of fruit. Serve immediately. Makes 12 servings.

Recipe developed by Lorie Hopcus for Stemilt Growers.

Easy Fruit Tarts
SunnyRidge/Dole Berry Company

Vegetable cooking spray

12 wonton skins

2 tablespoons apple jelly or apricot fruit spread

1½ cups sliced fruit, including Dole blueberries, strawberries, raspberries, blackberries, bananas, red or green seedless grapes

1 cup nonfat or low-fat vanilla yogurt

Preheat oven to 375°F.

Coat a 12-cup muffin pan with cooking spray.

Press 1 wonton skin into each muffin cup, allowing the corners to extend over the edges.

Bake for 6-8 minutes, or until lightly browned. Carefully remove the wonton cups to a wire rack; let cool.

In a small saucepan, cook jelly over low heat, stirring, until it melts.

Brush the bottoms of the cooled wonton cups with melted jelly. Place 2 fruit pieces in each cup. Spoon a rounded tablespoonful of yogurt over the fruit. Garnish with additional fruit, if desired. Serve immediately. Makes 12 servings.

Chocolate Chip Raisin Croissant Puddings

Vie de France

1¼ cups milk

⅓ cup granulated sugar

½ teaspoon vanilla extract

1 large egg, beaten

3 Vie de France butter
croissants, cubed

2 tablespoons semisweet
chocolate chips

2 tablespoons raisins

VANILLA SAUCE

1 large egg, beaten

1 tablespoon light brown sugar

¼ cup granulated sugar

1 teaspoon melted butter

1 teaspoon cornstarch

1 teaspoon vanilla extract

½ cup heavy cream

Pinch of ground cinnamon,
cloves and nutmeg

Grease a 12-cup muffin pan.

In a saucepan, heat milk, sugar and vanilla over low heat until bubbles appear, 4-5 minutes. Remove from the heat and stir in beaten egg until well blended. Set the batter aside.

In a large bowl, mix croissant cubes with chocolate chips and raisins. Place equal amounts of the croissant mixture in the muffin cups, then press gently. Pour batter into each cup; then let the batter soak into the puddings for 20 minutes. Preheat oven to 325°F.

Set the muffin pan in a slightly larger pan and add enough hot water to reach halfway up the sides of the muffin pan. Bake for 13-14 minutes, or until golden brown and no liquid appears when the tops are pressed.

Prepare the sauce: Combine all ingredients in the top of a double boiler. Cook over simmering water, stirring constantly, until it thickens.

Remove the puddings from the pan and serve with warm vanilla sauce. Makes 12 servings.

Strawberry Kuchen
Naturipe

1½ cups sliced Naturipe strawberries

⅔ cup sugar, divided

⅓ cup orange juice

1½ cups butter, room temperature

2 large eggs

2 cups flour

1½ teaspoons baking powder

1½ teaspoons ground cardamon

2 tablespoons plain yogurt

½ cup milk

Confectioners' sugar, for dusting

Sliced strawberries and chocolate curls, for garnish

Preheat oven to 325°F. Butter and flour a 9-inch springform pan.

In a saucepan, combine strawberries, ⅓ cup sugar and orange juice. Simmer until the strawberries are tender, about 10 minutes. Remove from the heat to cool.

Cream together butter and ⅓ cup sugar. Beat in eggs one at a time.

Sift all dry ingredients together. Combine yogurt and milk. Mix dry and wet ingredients into the batter, alternating wet and dry, beating until the batter is smooth and thick.

Pour the batter into the prepared pan. Spoon the strawberry mixture onto the batter.

Place a piece of foil under the pan to catch any drippings. Bake for 30 minutes, or until the top is golden brown. Let cool.

To serve, garnish with a dusting of confectioners' sugar, strawberry slices and chocolate curls. Makes 8-12 servings.

Peach and Nectarine Hazelnut Galette
Pride Packing Co./Fruit Patch

1 pound Mary's Pride peaches, skin removed

1 pound Fruit Patch nectarines

½ cup toasted hazelnuts

¼ cup sugar

2 tablespoons all-purpose flour

3 tablespoons unsalted butter, softened

1 large egg, lightly beaten

½ teaspoon vanilla extract

1 sheet frozen puff pastry, thawed

¼ cup peach preserves, warmed and strained

Vanilla ice cream or whipped cream, for serving

Preheat oven to 400°F.

Halve, pit and cut peaches and nectarines into ¼-inch-thick slices.

In a food processor, pulse hazelnuts, sugar and flour until finely ground.

In a medium bowl with an electric mixer, beat butter until light and fluffy (about 1 minute). Beat in egg and vanilla. Add the hazelnut mixture.

Unfold pastry onto a parchment-lined rimmed baking sheet. Spread the hazelnut mixture on the pastry, leaving a ½-inch border. "Shingle" the fruit slices over the hazelnut mixture.

Bake for about 35 minutes, or until the pastry is golden and puffed and the fruit is tender. (If bubbles form in the pastry, prick with a knife tip.) Brush the fruit with preserves and let cool for 20 minutes. Makes 8 servings.

Tip: Top with ice cream or whipped cream.

Three-Berry Tart
Kirkland Signature/Rader Farms

4 large eggs

¾ cup sugar

2 cups frozen Rader Farms/ Kirkland Signature Nature's Three Berries, divided

Grated zest and juice of ½ lemon

4 tablespoons heavy cream

CRUST

2½ cups flour

1 teaspoon salt

1 teaspoon sugar

1 cup cold butter, cut in small pieces

¼-½ cup ice water

1 egg, beaten

Prepare the crust: In a food processor, blend flour, salt and sugar. Add butter and pulse. Add water until dough is sticky. Wrap in plastic and chill for 1 hour.

Preheat oven to 425°F. Spray a 9-inch tart pan. Press crust mixture into pan. Line with parchment, add weights or beans, and bake until the edge begins to color, 20-25 minutes.

Reduce oven to 400°F. Remove parchment and weights, brush with egg and bake until golden, 15-20 minutes.

For the filling, whisk eggs and sugar in a mixing bowl. Puree 1 cup berries in a blender; stir into egg mixture. Add lemon zest, juice and cream; mix well. Arrange remaining berries on the crust, pour in filling, and bake until filling is set, 40 minutes. Let cool on a rack. Makes 8-10 servings.

Peaches and Custard Crème Tart (Gluten and Grain Free)
Kingsburg Orchards

3 extra-large egg yolks

½ cup milk

¼ cup sugar

2-3 Kingsburg Orchards peaches, peeled, pitted and thinly sliced

Almond slices (optional)

CRUST

2 cups almond meal, or 2 cups ground blanched almonds

⅓ cup butter, melted

¼ teaspoon ground cinnamon

1 teaspoon vanilla extract

Preheat oven to 350°F.

Prepare the crust: In a bowl, mix together almond meal, butter, cinnamon and vanilla with a fork. The mixture will be crumbly, but it will hold together when pressed down.

Press this mixture evenly into an 8-inch glass pie pan, or a 9-inch tart pan with a removable bottom. The crust should be about ¼ to ⅜ inch thick.

Bake for 10 minutes to set the crust.

Meanwhile, slowly whisk together egg yolks, milk and sugar. You want to mix it slowly so that air bubbles do not form, as that can give the custard a grainy texture.

When the crust is done, pour in the custard and bake for about 15-20 minutes. The custard should be soft-set—not runny, but still jiggles when you shake the pan a bit.

Layer the peaches to cover the top. Bake for another 5 minutes.

Let cool on the counter for 20-30 minutes.

Can be served warm, or chilled in the refrigerator before serving. Garnish with almond slices if desired. Makes 8-12 servings.

Cherry Hand Pies
Morada Produce

3 cups pitted and halved
  Morada Produce Bing cherries

¾ cup granulated sugar

3 tablespoons quick-cooking tapioca

Pinch of salt

1 tablespoon fresh lemon juice

1 teaspoon almond extract

2 egg whites

2 tablespoons water

1 package refrigerated pie dough

DRIZZLE

1 cup confectioners' sugar

¼ teaspoon vanilla extract

1 tablespoon milk

1 teaspoon fresh lemon juice

In a bowl, combine cherries, sugar, tapioca, salt, lemon juice and almond extract. Let sit for 30 minutes.

Preheat oven to 400°F. Line a baking sheet with parchment paper.

Whisk the egg whites and water together. Cut twelve 4-inch circles from the pie dough. Place a small amount of filling on each circle. Fold and pinch the edges together, creating mini turnovers. Brush the top of each hand pie with egg wash.

Press the sealed edges with the back of a fork to seal completely. Cut 3 small slits on the top of each hand pie.

Place the pies on the prepared baking sheet. Bake for 15-18 minutes, or until golden brown. Remove to a rack to cool.

When the pies are cooled completely, prepare the drizzle: In a small bowl, mix all ingredients together with a fork until smooth. Drizzle icing over each hand pie and serve. Makes 12 servings.

MORADA
Produce Company

Blueberry Stacks "4" My Boys

Townsend Farms

5 cups Townsend Farms fresh or frozen blueberries

1 tablespoon sugar

2 tablespoons orange juice concentrate, thawed

1 17.3-ounce package frozen puff pastry, thawed

½ teaspoon ground cinnamon plus ½ teaspoon sugar, blended

1 12-ounce container frozen whipped dessert topping, partially thawed and stirred

1 12-ounce bottle blueberry syrup

Preheat oven to 400°F. In a medium bowl, mix blueberries with sugar and orange juice. Set aside.

Unfold pastry sheets and cut at the folds for 6 rectangles per sheet. Place on a baking sheet. Sprinkle with the cinnamon sugar mix. Bake for 10-12 minutes, or until golden and puffed. Remove from the oven and gently press to flatten slightly. Cool on the pan for 10 minutes, then remove to a wire rack and cool completely.

For each serving, place 1 pastry rectangle on a serving platter. Leaving a ½-inch border, spread with whipped topping. Arrange some of the blueberry mixture evenly on top. Repeat with another 2 layers. Drizzle with blueberry syrup.

Chill for 10 minutes. Makes 4 servings.

Fruit Pizza
HMC Farms/Sequoia Orange

1 18-ounce package sugar cookie dough

8 ounces cream cheese, softened

1 cup sugar

1 large peach, sliced

1 large orange, sectioned

½ pint fresh strawberries, trimmed and sliced

6 ounces fresh blueberries

5 ounces fresh blackberries

½ cup chopped pecans

Preheat oven to 350°F.

Flatten the cookie dough to a 12-inch circle on a 14- to 16-inch pizza baking sheet. Bake the dough until firm, about 12-14 minutes. Let cool.

In a medium bowl, combine cream cheese and sugar; mix well.

Spread the cream cheese mixture onto the baked cookie. Decorate with sliced fruit. Top with berries and pecans. Cut into wedges. Makes 8 servings.

Caramelized Pears with Pomegranate Sauce
Trinity Fruit

4 Bartlett pears

1 pomegranate

¼ cup butter

½ cup sugar

Pinch of salt

8 mint leaves, for garnish

POMEGRANATE SAUCE

1 cup pomegranate juice

½ cup balsamic vinegar

Prepare the sauce: Cook juice and vinegar in a double boiler over boiling water until it thickens.

Peel, core and cut pears in half. Place in cold water to cover.

Open pomegranate and separate arils (seeds).

Preheat oven to 400°F.

While the sauce is thickening, place butter, sugar and salt in a 10-inch cast-iron pan. Bring to a boil over medium-low heat and cook, stirring and scraping the bottom, until the sugar caramelizes.

Place the 8 pear halves flat-side down in the pan and baste with the caramelized sugar. Cover the pan and bake for 30 minutes, or until the pears are tender.

Remove from the oven and let stand for 10 minutes. Serve warm, basting the pears with the caramelized sugar and drizzling with pomegranate sauce. Spread pomegranate arils around the pears and garnish with mint leaves. Makes 8 servings.

Recipe developed by Igal Treibatch.

Grilled Apricots à la Mode

Quick & Easy

Kingsburg Orchards

1 Kingsburg Orchards apricot per person

Olive or canola oil

Honey, about 1 tablespoon per apricot

Vanilla bean ice cream, for serving

Heat the grill to allow for direct medium-high heat.

Slice apricots into halves and remove the pits.

Lightly coat the apricots with oil to prevent them from sticking to the grill. Place on the grill cut-side down and grill for 1-2 minutes. This will soften the fruit, so take care when flipping them over.

Flip the fruit over so the skin side is now touching the grill. Grill for another 1-2 minutes, until warmed through but not falling apart. Slice apricots in half again, if desired.

Drizzle with honey and serve warm over ice cream.

Caramelized Grilled Pineapple

Ready Pac

½ cup butter

1 cup packed dark brown sugar

⅔ cup orange juice

1 teaspoon ground cinnamon

¼ teaspoon salt

1 3-pound container Ready Pac Sliced Gold Pineapple

Oil

Vanilla ice cream, for serving

Preheat the grill to high.

In a saucepan, melt butter over medium heat. Add sugar, orange juice, cinnamon and salt. Heat for 1-2 minutes, or until the sugar is dissolved, stirring often.

Place pineapple spears, flat side down, in a single layer in a shallow glass baking dish. Pour the hot sugar/butter mixture over the pineapple, turning once to coat all sides. Let stand for 10 minutes.

Reduce the grill heat to low. Brush the grates lightly with oil.

Remove the pineapple spears from the sugar/butter mixture and place on the hot grates. Cook for 10-15 minutes, or until grill marks appear, turning once and basting with all but 1-2 tablespoons of the remaining sugar/butter mixture.

To serve, arrange 3-4 hot caramelized pineapple spears in a triangle in each bowl. Top with ice cream and drizzle with the remaining sugar/butter mixture. Makes 4-6 servings.

Grape Clusters

Stevco

2 pounds seedless grapes,
  red or green

1 pound premium white baking
  chocolate, coarsely chopped

2 cups honey-roasted cashews,
  finely chopped

Fresh grape leaves,
  for garnish (optional)

Rinse grapes and drain well. Cut into clusters of 3. Set on paper towels and let dry completely.

Melt chocolate in the top of a double boiler over hot water. When completely melted, remove from the heat. Place cashews in a shallow bowl.

Holding the grape clusters by the stem, dip in the chocolate and allow excess to drain back into the pan.

Roll the grapes gently in the cashews. Place the grapes, stem side up, on waxed paper.

Refrigerate until firm. Serve within 4 hours. Garnish with grape leaves if desired. Makes 4-6 servings.

Fig Ambrosia

Cecelia Packing Corp./Earth Source Trading/Western Fresh Marketing

2 cups Cecelia Cara Cara orange sections

1 cup sliced fresh figs, any variety

2 tablespoons juice from Earth Source Trading lime

Sugar

½ cup flaked sweetened coconut

In a serving bowl, combine oranges, figs and lime juice. Add a little sugar to taste. Sprinkle with coconut. Keep refrigerated until serving time. Makes 4 servings.

Fresh Figs and Gingered Mascarpone

Stellar Distributing

1 cup mascarpone cheese (8½ ounces)

1 tablespoon finely chopped crystallized ginger

2½ tablespoons sugar

⅛ teaspoon vanilla extract

24 small firm-ripe fresh California figs (1½ pounds)

Mint sprigs, for garnish

Sweet round crackers or vanilla wafers, for serving

In a small bowl, stir together mascarpone, ginger, sugar and vanilla. Cover and chill.

To serve, scoop the mascarpone mixture onto a cold plate. Surround with figs. Garnish with mint sprigs and serve with sweet crackers or wafers. Makes 24 servings.

Note: For individual appetizers, spread the mascarpone mixture on crackers. Slice the figs and arrange on top. Dust with confectioners' sugar and garnish with mint sprigs.

Nectarines with Late-Harvest Citrus Jelly

Farms Co.

4-5 nectarines, halved, pitted and cut into thin slices

½ cup fresh orange juice

5 mint leaves, thinly sliced

¼ cup light brown sugar

1 cup blueberries, for garnish

JELLY

1 bottle (750 ml) late-harvest or sweet wine, such as Riesling

½ teaspoon grated orange zest

½ teaspoon grated lemon zest

¾ cup cold water

2 tablespoons gelatin

Prepare the jelly: In a large bowl, combine wine and orange and lemon zest. Pour cold water into a small saucepan; sprinkle with gelatin and let stand until it softens, about 5 minutes. Stir over medium-low heat just until the gelatin has dissolved, about 5 minutes (do not boil). Whisk into the wine. Pour into a 13-by-9½-inch rimmed sheet pan. Cover and refrigerate for at least 3 hours. (Can be made up to 2 days ahead. Keep refrigerated.)

In a large bowl, combine nectarines, orange juice, mint and sugar; toss to blend. Let stand, refrigerated, until the sugar dissolves, about 30 minutes.

Cut the jelly into bite-size pieces (about ½ inch square). Divide the fruit among 4-6 serving bowls. Put jelly cubes on top. Garnish with blueberries. Serve immediately. Makes 4-6 servings.

Fruit 'n' Pudding Parfaits

Sunkist Growers

1 package (4 servings) vanilla or chocolate instant pudding and pie filling (see note)

2 cups low-fat milk

Grated zest from 1 Sunkist orange

2 Sunkist oranges, peeled and cut into bite-size pieces

1 cup Sunkist green seedless grapes, cut in half

2 tablespoons chopped nuts

Prepare pudding with cold milk according to package directions. Stir in orange zest. Let stand for 5 minutes to thicken.

For each serving, spoon ¼ cup pudding into a parfait glass. Add ¼ of the orange pieces and grape halves. Top with ¼ cup more pudding. Sprinkle with chopped nuts. Makes 4 servings.

Note: One package of regular cooked pudding, prepared with milk and grated orange zest, can be substituted. It must be chilled thoroughly before assembling the parfaits.

Sunkist

Grape, Orange and Kiwi Jewel Parfaits

Quick & Easy

Unifrutti of America/Castle Rock Vineyards

4 South African navel oranges, peeled

2 cups Chilean or Californian grapes, halved or quartered

6 Grecian kiwifruit, peeled and cut into ½-inch pieces

24 ounces Greek yogurt (honey or honey-vanilla flavor)

2 cups Kirkland Signature Ancient Grains Granola with Almonds

Cut 3 oranges into ½-inch pieces. Cut 1 orange into slices.

In a bowl, combine the diced oranges with the grapes and kiwis. Reserve the orange slices.

In parfait glasses, begin with a layer of mixed fruit, then yogurt and then granola. Repeat the layering, reserving some of the fruit "jewels" to garnish the top. Finish with a dollop of yogurt, sprinkle with fruit and garnish with orange slices or half slices. Makes 6-8 servings.

Recipe developed by Christine W. Jackson, food stylist.

Clementine Jelly

AMC Direct

2 clementines, segmented

**4 gelatin sheets
(see note) or 1 teaspoon
unflavored gelatin**

**2¼ pounds clementines,
juiced (20 ounces
of juice), divided**

Juice of 1 lemon

2 teaspoons sugar, divided

**Whipped cream or
ice cream, for serving**

Place the segments of 1 clementine in the bottom of a 6- to 7-inch jelly mold or bowl.

Soften 2 sheets of gelatin in a little water. Add to this 10 ounces of warm (not hot) clementine juice, plus half of the lemon juice and 1 teaspoon sugar. Stir until the gelatin is dissolved. Pour over the clementine segments and place in the fridge to cool and set. Once it is set, place the segments of the second clementine on top.

Repeat the process of dissolving 2 sheets of gelatin in a little water with warmed clementine juice, lemon juice and 1 teaspoon sugar. Let cool a little, then pour over the top of the second clementine. Return to the fridge to set.

Once set, dip the mold in hot water and unmold the jelly. Serve with a spoonful of whipped cream or ice cream. Makes 2-4 servings.

Note: Gelatin sheets give a clearer consistency to the jelly; however, they are typically available only at food service retailers.

Perfect Peach Pound Cake

Sunny Valley International

1 cup butter, softened

3 cups granulated sugar

6 large eggs

1 teaspoon vanilla extract

½ teaspoon almond extract

3 cups flour

¼ teaspoon baking soda

½ cup sour cream

**2 cups finely diced peeled
fresh Eastern peaches**

**Confectioners' sugar,
for dusting**

**2 fresh Eastern peaches,
pitted and sliced,
for serving**

Preheat oven to 350°F. Grease and flour a 10-inch tube pan.

Cream butter and sugar with a mixer. Add eggs one at a time, beating well after each addition. Add vanilla and almond extracts and mix until blended.

In a small bowl, combine flour and baking soda. Add to the butter mixture and mix until incorporated.

Fold in sour cream and diced peaches. Pour into the tube pan.

Bake for 75-85 minutes, or until a toothpick inserted in the center comes out clean. Let cool for 30 minutes.

Remove the cake from the pan and sprinkle with confectioners' sugar. Serve with peach slices. Makes 6-8 servings.

Apple-Cardamom Cake with Cider Glaze
Domex Superfresh Growers

1½ cups all-purpose flour

2 teaspoons baking powder

1¼ teaspoons ground cardamom

¼ teaspoon kosher salt

½ cup unsalted butter, at room temperature

¾ cup sugar

2 large eggs

½ teaspoon pure vanilla extract

1 Superfresh Growers Fuji apple, quartered and cored

CIDER GLAZE

½ cup top-quality apple cider

½ cup confectioners' sugar

Preheat oven to 350°F. Butter and flour a 9-inch round cake pan.

In a small bowl, stir together flour, baking powder, cardamom and salt.

Beat together butter and sugar in a large bowl with an electric mixer. Continue beating until lightened, about 2 minutes longer. Beat in eggs one at a time, scraping the bottom and sides of the bowl to ensure that the ingredients are well blended. Add vanilla and blend in.

Coarsely grate the apple and immediately stir into the batter. Scatter half of the flour mixture over and gently stir in, then repeat with the remaining flour. Spoon the batter into the prepared pan, spreading it out evenly. Bake until a toothpick inserted in the center comes out clean, about 30 minutes. Let cool slightly, then turn the cake out and set it right-side up on a wire rack to cool completely.

Prepare the glaze: In a small saucepan, boil cider over medium-high heat until reduced to 2 tablespoons, 4-5 minutes. Put confectioners' sugar in a small bowl, add the reduced cider and stir until smooth. Let cool.

Set the cake on a cake plate. Pour the glaze onto the center of the cake and spread it out using the back of a spoon, allowing some to drip down the sides of the cake. Makes 8 servings.

Plum Upside-Down Cake
WesPak

PLUMS

1 tablespoon butter

4 large, firm, ripe WesPak plums, each cut into 8 wedges

¼ cup sugar

CAKE

1 cup all-purpose flour

¾ teaspoon baking powder

¼ teaspoon baking soda

¼ teaspoon salt

½ cup butter, softened

⅔ cup sugar

1 large egg

⅔ cup sour cream

1 teaspoon vanilla extract

Preheat oven to 350°F. Butter an 8-inch round cake pan and line with parchment paper.

Prepare the plums: Melt butter in a large skillet over medium-high heat. Add plums and sugar. Cook for 3-4 minutes, tossing until the sugar dissolves and juices become syrupy. Starting from the outside edge, arrange the plums in the pan, overlapping slightly. Pour the pan juices over the fruit.

Prepare the cake: Whisk together flour, baking powder, baking soda and salt.

In another bowl, beat butter and sugar until fluffy. Beat in egg, sour cream and vanilla. Gradually add the flour mixture, incorporating gently. Pour the batter over the plums.

Bake for 50 minutes, or until a toothpick inserted in the center comes out clean. Let cool in the pan for 1 hour, then invert onto a serving plate. Makes 6-8 servings.

Gooey Butter Cake with Dried Blueberries

Kirkland Signature/Meduri Farms

1 18¼-ounce package
  yellow cake mix
1 large egg
8 tablespoons butter, melted

FILLING

8 ounces cream cheese, softened
2 large eggs
1 teaspoon vanilla extract
8 tablespoons butter, melted
1 20-ounce bag Kirkland Signature
  dried blueberries
1 16-ounce box confectioners' sugar

Preheat oven to 350°F. Lightly grease a 13-by-9-inch baking pan.

In a mixing bowl, combine cake mix, egg and melted butter. Mix well with an electric beater. Pat the mixture into the bottom of the prepared pan.

Prepare the filling: In a large bowl, beat cream cheese until smooth. Add eggs, vanilla and melted butter; beat until blended. Stir in dried blueberries. Add sugar and mix until well blended.

Spread the filling over the cake batter. Bake for 40-50 minutes. Do not overbake—the center should be a little gooey.

Serve at room temperature. Makes 6-8 servings.

Citrus Mini Pound Cakes
Kings River Packing

1 16-ounce package pound cake mix

⅔ cup milk or water

3 eggs

¼ cup butter, softened

LEMON/ORANGE CAKES

Grated zest and juice of 1 lemon

2 teaspoons lemon extract

1 2- to 3-ounce package instant lemon pudding

⅓ cup milk

1 tablespoon poppy seeds (optional)

Grated zest of 1 orange

1-2 teaspoons orange extract

3-4 navel oranges, segmented by the supreme method (see note)

½ cup finely chopped pecans (optional)

ICING

½ cup butter, softened

2 tablespoons milk

1 pound confectioners' sugar

1 tablespoon lemon juice

2 teaspoons lemon extract

1 teaspoon orange extract

Preheat oven to 350°F. Grease 20-24 muffin cups or line with paper liners.

Follow package directions for mixing cake mix, milk (or water), eggs and butter. Divide equally between 2 bowls. For lemon pound cakes, add lemon zest, juice and extract, pudding, milk and poppy seeds; mix well. For orange pound cakes, add orange zest and extract; mix well. Chop half of oranges into ½-inch bits. Add to the batter with pecans.

Fill muffin cups ¾ full. Bake for 25-28 minutes, or until an inserted toothpick comes out clean. Cool completely before icing.

Prepare the icing: Beat butter, milk and sugar until smooth. Add lemon juice and extract to half of the icing. Add orange extract to remaining icing. Pipe onto the cupcakes. Garnish orange-flavored cakes with reserved segments. Makes 20-24 mini pound cakes.

Note: To supreme oranges, remove the skin by cutting off the top, bottom and sides of the orange, leaving no pith or outer membrane. Separate segments by cutting between the membranes with a sharp paring knife.

Recipe developed by Christine W. Jackson, food stylist.

Katie's Cherry Almond Cupcakes
Delta Packing Company

2 cups flour

1 teaspoon baking powder

¼ teaspoon baking soda

½ teaspoon salt

¾ cup buttermilk

⅓ cup cherry juice

½ cup butter

1½ cups sugar

1 teaspoon vanilla extract

½ teaspoon almond extract

4 egg whites

¼ cup chopped Delta Fresh cherries

FROSTING

½ cup butter

4 cups confectioners' sugar, divided

3 tablespoons cherry juice

1 teaspoon almond extract

¼ cup chopped Delta Fresh cherries

Preheat oven to 350°F. Grease a 12-cup cupcake pan.

Sift flour, baking powder, baking soda and salt. In a separate bowl, mix buttermilk and cherry juice.

Beat butter and sugar until fluffy. Add vanilla and almond extracts. Blend in egg whites one at a time, then beat for 1 minute. Blend in ⅓ of flour mixture, then ⅓ of buttermilk mixture. Repeat, alternating flour and buttermilk mixtures. Beat for 2 minutes. Fold in cherries.

Fill cupcake cups ⅔ full. Bake for 15-20 minutes.

Prepare the frosting: Cream butter and 1 cup sugar. Blend in cherry juice and almond extract. Add remaining sugar and beat for 2 minutes. Stir in cherries.

Frost the cooled cupcakes. Makes 12 servings.

DELTA
FRESH

One-Bowl Syrup Cake
The Hershey Company

½ cup (1 stick) butter or margarine, softened
1 cup sugar
4 large eggs
1¼ cups all-purpose flour
¼ teaspoon baking soda
1½ cups Hershey's Syrup

Preheat oven to 350°F. Grease a 13-by-9-by-2-inch baking pan.

In a large bowl, beat butter, sugar and eggs until thoroughly blended. Add flour and baking soda, blending well. Add syrup and mix thoroughly. Spread the batter in the prepared pan.

Bake for 35-40 minutes, or until a wooden pick inserted in the center comes out clean. Cool completely in the pan on a wire rack.

Top with your favorite frosting and garnishes, if desired. Makes 8-10 servings.

Red Velvet Cake with Warm White Chocolate-Sour Cream Sauce
Daisy Brand/Rich Products

⅔ cup white chocolate baking chips
2 cups Daisy Brand Sour Cream, divided
1 teaspoon vanilla extract
1 10-inch Kirkland Signature red velvet cake, cut into 16 slices

In a large microwavable bowl, combine baking chips and 1 cup of the sour cream. Microwave on high for 30 seconds; stir with a whisk. Continue to microwave in 15-second increments, whisking the mixture until it is smooth (see note).

Whisk in the remaining sour cream and vanilla until smooth. Microwave on high for 30-60 seconds, or until warm, whisking once.

To serve, drizzle 2 tablespoons of the sauce on each dessert plate. Place a slice of cake on top. Makes 16 servings.

Note: High-wattage microwaves may require less cooking time. Take care not to overcook.

Tip: Store leftover sauce, covered, in the refrigerator. Reheat as necessary for a few seconds in the microwave.

Dark Chocolate Almond Cherry Tortes

Kirkland Signature/Kerry

1 pound (about 28 pieces)
  Kirkland Signature Dark
  Chocolate Almond Cherry
  Clusters, coarsely chopped

1 cup unsalted butter

1 cup sugar

½ teaspoon salt

1 tablespoon vanilla extract

6 large eggs

¼ cup flour

RASPBERRY SAUCE

2 cups fresh or frozen raspberries

½ cup sugar

1 tablespoon lemon juice

Preheat oven to 325°F. Butter and flour two 9-inch round cake pans.

Heat water in a double boiler over medium heat until hot but not boiling. Place chocolate clusters and butter in the top of the double boiler and melt, stirring with a rubber spatula. Once melted, turn off the heat.

Stir in sugar, salt and vanilla. Add eggs one at a time, whisking after each addition. Gradually stir in flour. Divide the mixture between the prepared pans.

Bake for 18-22 minutes, or until the center is firm to the touch. Let cool for 20 minutes.

Prepare the sauce: Combine raspberries and sugar in a saucepan over medium-high heat. Bring to a boil, then reduce the heat and simmer, stirring occasionally, until the mixture starts to thicken, about 15 minutes. Press through a mesh strainer, using a spatula to extract as much liquid as possible. Discard seeds and skins. Stir in lemon juice. Add more sugar or lemon juice if desired. Serve warm or at room temperature.

Drizzle sauce on each slice and top with a chocolate cluster. Makes 12 servings.

Note: The raspberry sauce will keep for a week, tightly covered, in the refrigerator. You can gently reheat it before serving.

Apple-Pear Golden Brownies
Oneonta Starr Ranch Growers

1 cup packed light
   brown sugar

½ cup butter, melted

1 large egg

2 Starr Ranch Growers
   Gala or Pink Lady apples

1 Diamond Starr Growers
   Bosc pear

½ cup toffee chips

½ teaspoon vanilla extract

1 cup all-purpose flour

¼ teaspoon salt

½ teaspoon baking powder

½ teaspoon baking soda

½ teaspoon
   ground cinnamon

Vanilla ice cream, for serving

Preheat oven to 350°F. Grease a 9-by-9-inch baking pan.

In a large bowl, mix sugar, melted butter and egg until fluffy.

Peel and core apples and pear, then cut into small cubes. Fold into the egg mixture, along with toffee chips and vanilla.

In a separate bowl, sift together flour, salt, baking powder, baking soda and cinnamon. Stir the dry mixture into the wet mixture until just blended. Spread the batter evenly in the prepared pan.

Bake for 35 minutes, or until a toothpick inserted in the center comes out clean. Remove from the oven and let stand for 5 minutes before cutting into squares.

Serve with ice cream. Makes 9 servings.

ONEONTA
STARR RANCH
growers

Harvest Fruit Bars
Quaker/Tropicana

1 7-ounce package diced
   dried mixed fruit bits

1 cup chopped banana
   (about 2 medium)

⅔ cup Tropicana
   orange juice*

1½ teaspoons apple
   pie spice or ground
   cinnamon, divided

1¾ cups whole-wheat
   or all-purpose flour

1½ cups Quaker Oats
   (quick or old-fashioned,
   uncooked)*

½ pound butter, softened

1 cup firmly packed
   brown sugar

½ cup chopped nuts

Preheat oven to 375°F.

In a medium bowl, blend dried fruit, banana, juice and 1 teaspoon apple pie spice.

In another bowl, blend flour, oats and ½ teaspoon apple pie spice.

In a large bowl, beat butter and sugar with an electric mixer until creamy. Add oat mixture; beat until crumbly. Reserve ¾ cup for topping. Press remaining oat mixture into a 13-by-9-inch baking pan. Bake for 13-15 minutes, or until light golden brown.

Spread fruit evenly over crust to within ¼ inch of edge. Add nuts to the reserved oat mixture; mix well. Sprinkle evenly over fruit; pat down lightly.

Bake for 16-20 minutes, or until golden brown. Cool completely; cut into bars. Makes 10-12 servings.

* If using old-fashioned oats, decrease orange juice to ½ cup.

QUAKER   Tropicana

French Apple Slices
Yakima Fresh

All-purpose cooking spray

3 large eggs

1½ cups granulated sugar

1 tablespoon flour

3 tablespoons apple juice

4 large Yakima Fresh Gala apples

¾ cup chopped pecans

Confectioners' sugar, for dusting

Vanilla ice cream, for serving

CRUST

¾ cup cold butter

⅓ cup confectioners' sugar

1½ cups sifted flour

Preheat oven to 350°F. Coat the bottom of a 13-by-9-inch baking pan with cooking spray.

Prepare the crust: Cream butter and sugar with an electric mixer. Add flour and mix until crumbly. Pat into the prepared pan. Bake for 30 minutes, or until light golden brown.

While the crust is baking, place eggs in a bowl and beat well. By hand, mix in sugar, flour and apple juice until well blended.

Peel, core, and chop apples into ¼-inch pieces.

Remove the crust from the oven, and top with the chopped apples and pecans. Pour the egg mixture over the top and return to the oven for 30 minutes, or until the topping is set.

Remove from the oven and sprinkle with confectioners' sugar.

Serve at room temperature or warm with vanilla ice cream. Makes 8-10 servings.

Lemon Meringue Bars
Sun-Maid Growers

1 cup butter or margarine, softened

1¾ cups sugar, divided

4 large eggs, separated

1¾ cups all-purpose flour

1 tablespoon grated lemon zest

1 tablespoon lemon juice

1 cup Sun-Maid Natural Raisins

½ cup chopped nuts

Preheat oven to 350°F.

In a bowl, combine butter, 1 cup sugar and egg yolks; beat until light and fluffy. Add flour and lemon zest; mix well. Press the dough into an ungreased 13-by-9-inch pan.

Bake for 15 minutes, or until the edges are lightly golden.

Meanwhile, in a medium bowl, beat egg whites until soft peaks form. Gradually beat in the remaining ¾ cup sugar until stiff peaks form and the mixture is glossy.

Fold in lemon juice, then raisins and nuts. Spread over the baked crust.

Return to the oven and bake an additional 25 minutes, or until lightly browned.

Cut into bars while warm. Makes 24 bars.

Chocolate Brownies with Peppermint Bark

Ghirardelli

1½ sticks unsalted butter

1½ cups Ghirardelli 60% Cacao Bittersweet Chocolate Chips

3 large eggs, at room temperature

1 cup sugar

¼ teaspoon salt

1 teaspoon vanilla extract

½ cup plus 2 tablespoons all-purpose flour

½ teaspoon baking powder

26 squares Ghirardelli Peppermint Bark, chopped (divided)

Preheat oven to 350°F. Line a 13-by-9-inch baking pan with foil and grease with pan spray.

In a double boiler over hot water, melt butter and chocolate chips.

In a bowl, whisk together eggs, sugar, salt and vanilla. Gently whisk into the chocolate mixture.

In a small bowl, sift flour and baking powder. Fold into the chocolate mixture. Spread half of the mixture in the prepared pan. Sprinkle with 8 squares of chopped peppermint bark. Top with the remaining batter and spread evenly.

Bake for 15-20 minutes, or until a toothpick inserted in the center comes out clean. Let cool for 10 minutes, then sprinkle the warm brownies with the remaining chopped peppermint bark. Let soften for 1 minute, then swirl the melting peppermint bark with a spatula or whisk. Refrigerate for 1 hour. Cut into squares. Makes 18 servings.

Cherry Mini Brownies
M&R Company

1 cup sugar
¼ cup cocoa
½ cup butter, melted
2 large eggs
¾ cup flour
¼ teaspoon salt

1 teaspoon
 vanilla extract
1 cup pitted and
 quartered or chopped
 M&R cherries
2 dozen M&R cherries,
 pitted, for garnish

ICING
½ cup butter
⅔ cup cocoa
3 cups confectioners' sugar
⅓ cup milk
1 tablespoon vanilla extract

Preheat oven to 350°F. Line 24-36 mini muffin pan cups with paper baking cups.

Mix sugar, cocoa and melted butter. Add eggs one at a time, beating well after each addition. Add flour and salt, mixing well. Stir in vanilla and quartered/chopped cherries. Fill the muffin cups ¾ full.

Bake for 20-25 minutes, or until a toothpick inserted in the center comes out clean. Cool in the pan on a rack for 10 minutes, then remove from the pan.

Prepare the icing: Melt butter, then stir in cocoa. Alternately add confectioners' sugar and milk, beating on medium, adding more milk if necessary for the desired piping consistency. Stir in vanilla.

Frost the brownies by piping on the icing. Top each with sliced cherries (chocolate-dipped optional). Makes 24-36 mini brownies.

Recipe developed by Christine W. Jackson, food stylist.

Chocolate Chunk Nut Clusters

Kirkland Signature/J&J Snack Foods

4 Kirkland Signature chocolate chunk cookies

1 cup chopped pecans or peanuts

1½ cups semisweet chocolate chips

1½ cups white chocolate chips or peanut butter chips

In a bowl, break cookies into large chunks. Add pecans and stir to blend.

Line a large cookie sheet with waxed paper.

In a large saucepan, combine semisweet chocolate and white chocolate chips. Melt over low heat.

Remove from the heat and immediately add the cookie/pecan mixture. Stir until well coated.

Working quickly, using a large serving spoon, drop spoonfuls of the mixture onto the cookie sheet, creating small piles.

When the chocolate is set, remove the clusters from the cookie sheet. Store in the refrigerator. Makes 12-15 servings.

Chocolate-Enrobed Cashew Clusters
Kirkland Signature

1 pound milk or dark chocolate chips

About 1 pound (½ bag) Kirkland Signature Cashew Clusters

Parchment or waxed paper

Double boiler method: Reserve ¼ cup of chocolate chips. Place remaining chocolate chips in a glass or metal mixing bowl on top of a pan half full of water. Heat the water over medium-high until it is steaming, but not boiling. For best results, bring the chocolate temperature up to 120°F, stirring frequently. Then reduce the heat and add about 10 of the reserved chips with every 10-degree drop. Once you reach 90°F, do not add more chips. The optimal temperature for dipping is 86°F. Caution: Never let the water come into contact with the chocolate.

Microwave method: Heat chocolate at 50% power, stirring every 30 seconds, until it is 120°F, liquid and no lumps. Reduce the heat and add the remaining chips as described above.

Using small tongs, carefully dip each cashew cluster halfway or fully into the melted chocolate, then set aside or refrigerate on parchment or waxed paper to cool and harden, about 45 minutes. Makes 32 clusters.

Coffee Gingerbread Truffles
Starbucks Coffee

¾ cup heavy cream

8 ounces bittersweet chocolate, finely chopped (approximately 1⅓ cups)

1 packet Starbucks VIA Ready Brew

1 teaspoon ground cinnamon

½ teaspoon ground ginger

¼ teaspoon ground cloves

¼ cup cocoa powder

Heat cream to just under a boil.

In a bowl, combine chopped chocolate, Starbucks VIA Ready Brew and spices. Pour the hot cream over the mixture and stir until the chocolate melts completely.

Spread the chocolate in a shallow pan and chill until firm but still scoopable.

To shape, place cocoa powder on a plate. Coat your hands with some cocoa.

Scoop the chocolate mixture with a teaspoon and shape into a ball. Roll in the cocoa and place on a clean plate.

Cover the truffles with plastic wrap. Refrigerate for up to a week. Makes 28-30 truffles.

Holiday Fondue with Fruitcake Pops
Dawn Food Products

½ cup heavy cream

12 ounces semisweet chocolate chips

2 tablespoons brandy (or rum)

¼ cup chopped toasted almonds

¼ cup shredded coconut

1 Kirkland Signature traditional fruitcake, cut into 1-inch cubes

Toothpicks

Bring cream to a boil in a small heavy saucepan. Turn off the heat and add chocolate and brandy. Stir until smooth. Pour into a fondue pot and keep warm.

To serve, place almonds and coconut in bowls. Skewer the fruitcake cubes with toothpicks. Dip into the warm fondue, then into the nuts or coconut. Makes 16 servings.

Variations

Grand Marnier: Replace brandy with Grand Marnier. Add grated zest of an orange.

White Chocolate: Replace semisweet chocolate with 14 ounces white chocolate. Omit the brandy.

Gianduja: Replace semisweet chocolate with 6 ounces dark chocolate. Replace brandy with Frangelico. Add ¼ cup Nutella.

Tuxedo Jelly Bean Fudge
Kirkland Signature/Jelly Belly

2 cups sugar, divided

1 teaspoon salt, divided

6 tablespoons unsalted butter, divided

1 cup heavy cream, divided

3½ cups mini marshmallows, divided

2 teaspoons pure vanilla extract, divided

1½ cups semisweet chocolate chips

1½ cups white chocolate chips

9 ounces Jelly Belly jelly beans

Line a 13-by-9-inch baking pan with waxed or parchment paper with the ends overhanging the sides; coat with cooking spray.

In a saucepan, combine half of the sugar, salt, butter, cream, marshmallows and vanilla. Cook over medium heat, stirring, until the butter and marshmallows are almost melted. Bring to a boil and cook, stirring occasionally, for 5 minutes. Remove from the heat. Add semisweet chocolate chips and stir until melted.

Pour into the lined pan. Cool until firm, 15 minutes.

Repeat the process with the remaining sugar, salt, butter, cream, marshmallows and vanilla, adding white chocolate chips. Pour over the chocolate layer. Refrigerate for 10 minutes.

Score the fudge into 1-inch squares. Press 2 jelly beans into each square.

Let cool in pan at room temperature for 3 hours. Remove by lifting paper from pan; cut fudge along scored lines. Makes 117 squares.

Grape Delight Cookies
Pandol Bros., Inc.

- 1½ cups confectioners' sugar
- 1 18.25-ounce package lemon cake mix
- 2 cups (6 ounces) whipped dessert topping
- 1 large egg
- 1 teaspoon rum extract
- 1 teaspoon vanilla extract
- 1½ cups chopped walnuts (optional)
- 2 cups Pandol red seedless grapes, diced (not necessary to remove skins)

Preheat oven to 350°F. Line a cookie sheet with parchment paper. Place confectioners' sugar in a shallow bowl.

With a spoon, mix together cake mix, whipped topping, egg and extracts. Fold in walnuts and grapes.

Drop by the spoonful into the confectioners' sugar and roll into 1½-inch-diameter balls.

Place on the cookie sheet 2 inches apart. Bake for 15 minutes, or until lightly browned. The cookies will be soft.

Slide the parchment paper (with cookies) off the cookie sheet to cool before serving. The cookies can be refrigerated. Makes 4 dozen cookies.

Recipe developed by Sherry Wysinger of Pandol.

Coffee Meringue Cookies
Starbucks Coffee

- 3 egg whites (about ½ cup)
- ½ teaspoon cream of tartar
- ¼ teaspoon salt
- 1 teaspoon vanilla extract
- ¾ cup sugar
- 1 packet Starbucks VIA Ready Brew

Preheat oven to 275°F. Line cookie sheets with parchment or foil.

In a large bowl, combine egg whites, cream of tartar, salt and vanilla. Beat until they stand in soft peaks.

Stir the sugar and Starbucks VIA Ready Brew together and slowly add to the whites, while continuing to beat until they stand in stiff peaks.

Shape the meringues on the parchment using a teaspoon. Form 1½-inch mounds about an inch apart.

Bake for about 30 minutes.

Let cool completely before storing. Makes 48 cookies.

Raspberry White Chocolate Cheesecake
Raskas

- 1 9-ounce package chocolate wafer cookies, crushed
- 3 tablespoons butter, melted
- 8 ounces white chocolate, broken into pieces
- 1½ pounds Raskas cream cheese, softened
- 1 cup sugar
- 4 large eggs
- 1 tablespoon vanilla extract
- 2 cups whipping cream, divided
- ⅔ cup raspberry jam
- ½ cup ground walnuts

Preheat oven to 325°F.

Mix cookie crumbs and butter. Press onto the bottom and partway up the sides of a 9-inch springform pan. Arrange chocolate pieces over the crust.

In an electric mixer, beat cream cheese and sugar until blended. Add eggs one at a time, beating well after each addition. Add vanilla and 1½ cups whipping cream. Beat at medium speed for 10 minutes.

Spoon ⅔ of the cream cheese mixture over the chocolate. Drop spoonfuls of jam on the mixture. Top with the remaining cream cheese mixture. Swirl a knife gently through the jam and cream cheese mixture for a marbling effect.

Bake for 1½ hours, or until set. Let cool, then refrigerate until chilled.

To serve, whip ½ cup cream, then pipe a border around the cake edges. Sprinkle with walnuts. Makes 8-12 servings.

Blackberry Silk Pie
Sun Belle

- 1 18-ounce container Sun Belle blackberries
- 1 teaspoon vanilla extract
- 2 tablespoons lemon juice
- 4 large egg yolks
- 1 14-ounce can sweetened condensed milk
- 1 9-inch graham cracker pie shell
- Lightly sweetened whipped cream, for garnish

Preheat oven to 350°F.

Reserve 8 blackberries for garnish. Place the remaining blackberries in a food mill or blender and puree. Press through a strainer to remove the seeds. Add vanilla and lemon juice to the puree.

In a bowl, beat egg yolks until pale yellow and creamy. Gradually add condensed milk to the yolks, beating until thickened.

Combine the blackberry puree and egg mixture. Pour into the pie shell.

Bake for 15 minutes, or until the filling is firm but still jiggly. Let cool on a rack, then refrigerate for at least 1 hour.

To serve, garnish with whipped cream and the reserved blackberries. Makes 8 servings.

Note: For a slightly tart taste, substitute fresh lime juice for the lemon juice.

Rice Pudding with Bourbon-Butter Sauce

Bunge Milling, Inc. d/b/a Pacific International Rice Mills, LLC

½ cup coconut milk

2 tablespoons light brown sugar

¼ teaspoon ground cinnamon,
    plus more to taste

¼ teaspoon vanilla extract

Pinch of fine sea salt,
    plus more for seasoning

1 cup cooked Homai Calrose rice

Maple sugar

BOURBON-BUTTER SAUCE

¼ cup butter

½ cup dark brown sugar, loosely packed

2 tablespoons Maker's Mark bourbon

¼ cup sweetened condensed milk

In a large saucepan, combine coconut milk, brown sugar, cinnamon, vanilla and salt. Heat over medium-high heat until the sugar and salt have dissolved. Add rice and stir to mix well. Cook until the rice mixture is heated through (150°F) and remove from the heat. Season to taste with maple sugar and cinnamon.

To serve, top the rice pudding with the sauce and serve hot, or refrigerate for a cool variation. Makes 3 servings.

Prepare the sauce: In a saucepan, combine butter and brown sugar; whisk over medium-high heat until combined. Add bourbon and mix well. Reduce the heat to low. Add condensed milk and cook until all the sugar has dissolved (180°F). Refrigerate if not ready to use immediately.

Rice Pudding with Cherry Sauce
Chelan Fresh Marketing

2 cups cold water

1 cup Arborio rice

3 cups milk

¼ cup sugar

Pinch of salt

½ teaspoon vanilla extract

½ teaspoon ground cinnamon

¼ teaspoon ground nutmeg

CHERRY SAUCE

1 cup Chelan Fresh sweet cherries (fresh or frozen), pitted

1 12-ounce jar cherry preserves

Grated zest of 1 lemon

Preheat oven to 375°F.

Bring the water to a boil in a medium-size heavy ovenproof saucepan. Add rice, cover and simmer for 20 minutes, or until the rice is nearly cooked.

Meanwhile, in a large bowl, whisk milk, sugar and salt. Stir into the hot rice. Cover, place in the oven and cook for 45 minutes.

Remove from the oven and stir in vanilla, cinnamon and nutmeg. The pudding will be slightly liquidy, but it will thicken as it cools.

Prepare the sauce: In a small saucepan, combine all ingredients and stir to blend. Heat to a simmer. Remove from the heat.

Divide the pudding among 8 bowls. Top with cherry sauce. Serve warm or at room temperature. Makes 8 servings.

Holiday Cherry Nut Snack Mix
General Mills

¼ cup sugar

½ teaspoon ground cinnamon

⅓ cup butter or margarine

1 cup Corn Chex cereal

1 cup Rice Chex cereal

1 cup Wheat Chex cereal

1 cup Chocolate Cheerios cereal

¾ cup toasted sliced almonds

1 cup dried banana chips

½ cup dried cherries

In a small bowl, mix sugar and cinnamon.

In a large microwavable bowl, microwave butter, uncovered, on high for about 40 seconds, or until melted. Stir in cereals and almonds until evenly coated. Microwave, uncovered, on high for 2 minutes, stirring after 1 minute.

Stir in the sugar mixture and banana chips until evenly coated. Microwave, uncovered, on high for 1 minute. Spread on paper towels to cool.

Place the mix in a serving bowl; stir in cherries. Store in an airtight container. Makes 14 servings.

Note: Other dried nuts and fruits can be substituted for the almonds, banana chips and cherries.

Nutritional information: Each ½-cup serving has 190 calories, 2 g protein, 22 g carbohydrates, 10 g fat, 10 mg cholesterol, 2 g fiber, 140 mg sodium, 10 g sugar.

Index

Supplier Listing

Cott Corporation, 44
www.cott.com
888-777-2389

CSM Bakery Products, 120, 121
www.csmbakeryproducts.com
800-241-8526

Curry & Company, 191
www.curryandco.com
503-393-6033

Cuties Clementine Cooperative, 12
www.CutiesKids.com
213-612-9957

D'Arrigo Bros. Co., of California, 77
www.andyboy.com
800-995-5939

Daisy Brand, 214
www.daisybrand.com
877-292-9830

Dawn Food Products, 18, 224
www.dawnfoods.com
800-292-1362

Decas Cranberry Products, 67
www.decascranberry.com
508-866-8506 x126

Del Monte Fresh Produce N.A., Inc., 124
www.freshdelmonte.com
800-950-3683

Del Rey Avocado, 154, 155
www.delreyavocado.com
760-728-8325

Delano Farms, 103, 104, 105
www.delanofarmsco.com
661-721-1485

Delta Packing Company, 213
www.deltapacking.com
209-334-1023

Diamond Foods, Inc., 22
www.diamondnuts.com
209-467-6000

Divine Flavor LLC, 23, 141
www.divineflavor.com
619-616-7410

Dole Berry Company, 197
www.dole.com

Dole Food Company, 51, 125
www.dole.com

Domex Superfresh Growers, 80, 210, 211
www.superfreshgrowers.com
509-966-1814

Don Miguel Mexican Foods, 40
www.donmiguel.com
972-246-3038

Dream Foods Int. LLC, 44
www.dreamfoods.com
877-9VOLCANO

Duda Farm Fresh Foods, Inc., 77, 152, 153
www.dudafresh.com
866-669-8166

Earth Source Trading, Inc., 206
www.earthsourcetrading.com
877-321-8200

Earthbound Farm, 98, 99
www.ebfarm.com
800-690-3200

Einstein Bros. Bagels, 184
www.einsteinbros.com
1-800-BAGEL-ME

Eurofresh Farms, 32
www.eurofresh.com
520-384-4621

Faribault Foods, Inc., 38
www.swbeans.com
877-331-9805

Farm Fresh Direct, 63
www.farmfreshdirect.com
719-852-2600

Farms Co. S.A., 207
www.farmsco.cl

Ferrero USA, 14
www.nutellausa.com

Fillmore Piru Citrus, 81, 132, 153, 155
www.fillmorepirucitrus.com
800-621-8465

First Fruits Marketing, 116, 117
www.firstfruits.com
509-853-4710

Florida Classic Growers, Inc., 64
www.flclassic.com
863-438-2200

Foodcomm Fresh & Natural, 181
www.foodcomm.com
800-445-4622

Foster Farms, 96, 97
www.fosterfarms.com
800-255-7227

Four Star Sales, 69, 74, 178
www.fourstarfruit.com
661-725-9621

Fowler Packing Co., 46
www.fowlerpacking.com

Freska Produce International, LLC, 25
www.freskaproduce.com
805-650-1040

Fruit Patch Sales, LLC, 199
www.fruitpatch.net
559-591-1170

Garofalo Pasta/P&L Imports, 90, 91, 92
www.pandlimports.com
866-327-2782

General Mills, 37, 229
www.bettycrocker.com
800-345-2443

Ghirardelli Chocolate Company, 220
www.ghirardelli.com
888-402-6262

Giorgio Fresh Co., 157
www.giorgiofoods.com
800-330-5711

Giumarra Agricom International, 154, 155
www.giumarra.com
760-480-8502

Gold Coast Packing, Inc., 58
www.goldcoastpack.com
805-928-2593

GoodHeart Brand Specialty Foods, 160
www.goodheart.com
210-637-1963

Gourmet Trading Company, 49, 191
www.gourmettrading.net

Greene River Marketing, 47
772-778-8403

Grimmway Farms, 42
www.grimmway.com
800-301-3101

Grower Direct Marketing LLC, 57
209-931-7900

Harvest Manor Farms, 187
www.hoodysnuts.com
800-445-8338 x525

Hershey Company, The, 214
www.hersheys.com
800-468-1714

Hickman's Family Farms, 17
www.hickmanseggs.com
623-872-1120

Hillandale Farms, 17
www.hillandalefarms.com
717-229-0601

HJ Heinz Company, 163, 168, 194
www.heinz.com
800-255-5750

HMC Farms, 203
www.hmcfarms.com
559-897-1025

Supplier Listing